1864
THE YEAR THAT CHANGED CRICKET

KIT HARRIS

WISDEN
Bloomsbury Publishing Plc
50 Bedford Square, London, WC1B 3DP, UK

Bloomsbury Publishing Ireland Limited
29 Earlsfort Terrace, Dublin 2, D02 AY28, Ireland

First published in Great Britain 2026

www.wisdenalmanack.com
Follow Wisden on X @WisdenAlmanack

A catalogue record for this book is available from the British Library
ISBN: HB: 978-1-3994-3507-9; eBook: 978-1-3994-3508-6

2 4 6 8 10 9 7 5 3 1

Typeset in Garamond
Printed and bound in Great Britain by Clays Ltd, Elcograf S.p.A

MIX
Paper | Supporting responsible forestry
FSC® C018072

To find out more about our authors and books visit www.wisdenalmanack.com and sign up for our newsletters.

For product-safety related questions, contact productsafety@bloomsbury.com.

1864
THE YEAR THAT CHANGED CRICKET

KIT HARRIS

W I S D E N

LONDON • OXFORD • NEW YORK • NEW DELHI • SYDNEY

CONTENTS

Match reports from the English first-class season, and the player profiles of England's touring team in Australia, are amalgamations of reports from *Bell's Life*, the *Evening Standard*, *Sporting Gazette* and *Sporting Life*.

ALSO BY THE AUTHOR

The Queen at the Cricket (2022)

From Lord's to the Fjords (2023)

The author would like to thank Philip Bailey, Stephen Baldwin, Allan Engel, David Frith, Matthew Hau, Nigel King, Bohdana Ladyrova, Daniel Lawrence, Katy McAdam, Daniel Norcross, Astrid Potter-Harris, Alan Rees, Chris Ridler, Alice Smith, and Steve Smith.

INTRODUCTION

The past is a foreign country. They play cricket differently there. The mid-nineteenth century was an era of underarm bowling, teams of twenty-two, beribboned hats, heeled boots and belted trousers.

Britain, too, would have been barely recognisable at the start of 1864 – and London in particular. The built-up area extended only to Paddington and Hackney in the north, Clapham and Camberwell in the south. The bastions of the modern suburbs – Hammersmith, Hampstead, Tottenham, Stratford, Greenwich, Lewisham, Dulwich and Putney – were villages surrounded by fields. The Underground, whose spreading branches would connect them all to the city centre, triggering rampant urban growth by the end of the century, was less than a year old, and less than four miles long.

Queen Victoria, aged 44, was still in mourning for her husband, Prince Albert, who had died three years earlier. Many cricketers remembered Albert fondly, since he had stepped in to prevent The Oval from being sold to housing developers in 1851. Victoria had only returned to public appearances in 1863, and would not be seen in London until June 1864. Her eldest son, the Prince of Wales – who would succeed her, aged 59, as Edward VII – was just 22.

The British Empire was still growing. Its main possessions were Australia, Canada, India, Ireland, New Zealand, Sri Lanka (then Ceylon) and most of the West Indies; by the end of the century, it would control all of what are now Pakistan, South Africa and Zimbabwe. Cricket was played in all those places, mainly by expat traders, Empire officials and garrisoned soldiers.

Everyday life in Britain was changing too. Leisure time and wages were increasing at all levels of the economy – though these levels were very far apart. Labourers and factory workers might earn £3 per month (£1 in 1864 would be worth about £110 in 2026), craftsmen and engineers £10, lawyers more than £60. A room in a slum cost about £1 per month, a terraced house in the suburbs £5, and a large house in a fashionable area £40. Per pound (450g), bread, milk and candles cost tuppence, beef, cheese and sugar sixpence, butter a shilling, tea two shillings. A work horse could be bought for £10.

Brighton, like many English towns, was undergoing rapid expansion, and the Wisden family were in the thick of it. They had transformed a bricklaying business into a prosperous housing development company, with at least five properties by the 1820s, and numerous contracts with the town council.

John Wisden was born in 1826, at 26 Crown Street (later renumbered to 32). As a young boy, he would run to Temple Field, less than half a mile to the north, where the veteran Sussex cricketer William Lillywhite, who had taken more than 2,000 wickets in his career, now ran a cricket school. Lillywhite's sons – James, John and Fred – were about the same age as Wisden, and they often played together while Lillywhite coached. If they were lucky, they would get sixpence for retrieving the balls after the session.

Wisden had less time for that when he turned 11, and was enrolled at Middle Street School, a few minutes from his home. Boys usually entered work aged 12, so it seems likely he only spent a year in education. On 5 September 1838, his twelfth birthday, Wisden was selected for Lillywhite's Brighton Under-14 team, against Lewes at Temple Field. James and John were also picked. Both brothers went on to play first-class cricket – John for 25 years – and their cousin, another James, would captain England in the first Test match. But there was little of the family talent on show against Lewes: the Brighton boys lost heavily.

Sometime in the early 1840s, the Wisdens left Crown Street, and moved to 2 Suffolk Place, nearer the centre of Brighton (the road was later renamed Cannon Street, and the site of the house now sits under Unit 46 of the Churchill Square shopping centre). Three years later, Lillywhite's ground was closed for the construction of Montpelier Crescent.

Wisden made his first class debut in 1845, aged 19, for Sussex against Kent at Brighton, taking nine wickets, including six for 46 in the first innings. Though only five feet four, and seven stone, he had a whippy roundarm action with a remarkable break from the off – some sources say as much as a yard. His debut came three years ahead of the young Lillywhites. Their father found coaching work at Cambridge University, and brought the lads with him to help. Wisden made a lot of prominent acquaintances, including Francis Cary Elwes, a sports-mad gentleman with a penchant for sporting facts and figures.

By August 1846, Wisden's prowess was sufficiently well known for MCC to select him for an England XI to face Kent at Canterbury. Among the XI were two Nottingham men: William Clarke, now 47, but still the greatest slow bowler in the country, and the young George Parr, who had arguably succeeded Kent's Fuller Pilch as the greatest batsman. During the match, Clarke finalised plans for a professional All England Eleven, who could be hired by any club to play against odds (in other words, the club could field up to 22 players) for a substantial fee. Clarke's team debuted at Sheffield at the end of the month, and Parr was soon persuaded to join.

The death of Wisden's father, William, in the spring of 1847, left a substantial estate, but since he had eight living children, probate took some time to sort out. John Wisden saw out the year with his first appearances for All England, top-scoring on his debut, against Yorkshire.

When All England played at Leamington, in September 1848, Clarke brought along Parr, plus Fred Lillywhite as scorer. Lillywhite had recently set up a scorecard-printing tent at Lord's, setting in train a career that would, within a decade, establish his name as cricket's foremost statistician and publisher. He had also started work on his *Guide to Cricketers*, which was first published the following year, and would become a best-selling almanack of the game. Lillywhite didn't think much of Leamington, though. "If the ground at Darlington was bad, it was beautiful compared with Leamington," he wrote. "For this was a few yards of mown and rolled grounds, in the midst of a ridge-and-furrow field."

Parr saw it differently, and suggested to Wisden that this was a golden opportunity to invest his inheritance. They went into partnership, leased the site – on Adelaide Road, between the railway and the river, and now known as Victoria Park – and moved to Leamington to develop it. By May 1849, Parr and Wisden's Cricket Ground was in excellent condition. That same year, Wisden became engaged to Parr's sister, Annie.

Leamington briefly became a hotbed of talent. Less than two years after mustering 165 runs for 41 wickets against All England on a farmer's field, a Leamington XI – including Parr and Wisden – beat MCC at Lord's.

That was 1850, Wisden's annus mirabilis. The first two weeks of July were the peak of his cricketing life. He was well past 100 wickets in the season when he arrived at Tunbridge Wells to play for Sussex against Kent, and he now hit his first century. He then travelled to Lord's, where he took four wickets in each innings for All England against Kent (dismissing the 46-year-old Pilch), then five in each innings (including his old mentor William Lillywhite twice) in the Leamington game. Next came the annual North v South fixture, which the North won by an innings – in a single day – when Wisden single-handedly dismissed the South in the second innings. All ten, all bowled.

During his time in London, Wisden often stayed with the Lillywhites, at 10 Princes Terrace in Islington where, that same year, they opened their first sporting goods shop (it lives on today at Piccadilly Circus). Here he saw, first hand, how cricketing commerce could flourish.

The All England side hit stormy weather in 1851. The players began expressing discontent with Clarke's authoritarian attitude, poor timekeeping, and selfish management of the finances. He charged clubs £70 for a fixture, and paid his players £4 each. This was a typical fee for a professional, but Clarke was certainly making a handsome profit. At the end of each game, he would sit at a table, calling and paying each man in turn, before sweeping the rest of the cash into his lap with a hearty "And £30 for me!" Things came to a head the following year, when Wisden began his own venture: the United England Eleven. To all intents and purposes, the concept was identical to Clarke's. It just didn't involve Clarke.

Needless to say, Clarke was furious. He pulled out of an All England match at Ilkeston, stormed to Newmarket, where United England were beginning their second game, and gave them the benefit of his opinion. Wisden's men were so offended they signed a declaration stating they would never play for Clarke again. An epistolary battle between the two captains continued, via the newspapers, well into 1853.

William Lillywhite died from cholera in 1854, tipping his sons into financial uncertainty. John decided to try and keep the shop afloat, while Fred decided to shore up his future by going into partnership with Wisden, who still had a sizeable chunk of his inheritance. By October 1855, they were running a cricket (and cigar) emporium, at 2 New Coventry Street in the middle of London. Lillywhite's *Guide to Cricketers* had now run to eight successful editions, so he and Wisden embarked on a gargantuan project, *Scores and Biographies*, intended as a definitive volume of historical matches.

Clarke's death, in 1856, put the All England team in the hands of the more open-minded Parr. He and Wisden – still lessees of the ground at Leamington – immediately buried the hatchet, and formed the Cricketers' Fund Friendly Society, to raise money for professionals who had fallen on hard times. Fred Lillywhite became the secretary, and the inaugural fixture between All England and United England, at Lord's on 1 June 1857, was the Fund's first benefit match.

Annie Parr died on 5 September, ending an eight-year, unfulfilled engagement. Wisden never married. Cricket was his mistress, and that relationship was flourishing. In 1858, Lillywhite & Wisden first advertised their patent Catapulta, a bowling machine modelled on a slingshot, which they had devised a few years earlier.

It came as a surprise when, on 18 January 1859, the *London Gazette* announced the dissolution of Lillywhite & Wisden. The reason has never been known, but subsequent writings – especially by Lillywhite – suggested a build-up of resentment. Lillywhite had always been jealous of Wisden's prosperity, which he felt was inherited, rather than earned. And Wisden had done little to help with *Scores and Biographies*, which was occupying more and more of Lillywhite's time. Wisden bought him out, and Lillywhite established his own premises at The Oval.

An already strained relationship soured further when the pair travelled to North America on the first international cricket tour, under the captaincy of Parr. Lillywhite brought his printing equipment and tent, which were so cumbersome – and Lillywhite so fussy about them – that the touring party were put to endless trouble. By the time they reached New York, Parr had had enough and, as one account put it, "in pretty plain language consigned both Lillywhite and his tent to an unmentionable region". In 1860, Lillywhite published a book about the tour, and made a point of thanking all the participants except Parr and Wisden: "No assistance has been received, in publishing this work, from either of the managers of the two celebrated Elevens."

Lillywhite spent most of 1861 trying to complete *Scores and Biographies*, but was now also bogged down with the *Guide*, which became a twice-yearly publication in 1862. *Scores and Biographies* was scheduled for May, then June, and finally came out in July; Lillywhite's reputation for reliability was shaken. His mood darkened, and gradually marginalised him.

The Cricketers' Fund Friendly Society decided that Wisden should take over from Lillywhite as secretary, but Lillywhite was having none of it. Only when legal proceedings were about to commence, in October 1863, did he co-operate, turning up at the court and thrusting fistfuls of the Society's papers into Wisden's hands.

Wisden had just played his final match, for United England at Alnwick (he scored nought and one, and did not bowl). But he would not be at a loose end. He now had the Society to run, a team to manage, a shop to oversee – and an almanack to assemble.

EMBARKATION

English cricketers had planned overseas tours before. In 1789, Chertsey Cricket Club despatched a team to play in Paris, where they were to be welcomed by the British ambassador, the Duke of Dorset. He showed up earlier than expected – at Dover, fleeing the French Revolution. No boats were boarded that year.

Subsequent plans proved more fruitful. In September 1859, as the home season drew to a close, a squad of twelve – organised by Parr, with the assistance of Wisden and Lillywhite, in the wake of the break-up of their business partnership – had set sail from Liverpool for five matches in Canada and the USA. They played twice each at Montreal, New York and Philadelphia, then returned to Canada for three more games, in Hamilton and Rochester, before sailing home.

Six of Parr's squad were from the All England roster, and six from United England; they were the cream of cricketing talent. Not only did they go through the tour unbeaten – indeed, they were so strong, their opponents never fielded fewer than 22 players – but some demonstrated astounding skill. Tom Lockyer, the wicketkeeper, gathered throws from the outfield and rifled the ball back to the bowler with such fluidity and accuracy that the crowds applauded him every time he did it. Tom Hayward, when fielding in the covers, routinely ran batsmen out by pretending to have misfielded. Wisden took six wickets in six balls at Rochester.

Unexpected talents were exhibited, too. Bob Carpenter entertained the passengers with heartfelt renditions of 'The Sweet Cherub That Sits Up Aloft', the only song he knew. John Jackson celebrated each of his wickets by blowing his nose so loudly he earned the nickname 'Foghorn'. Billy Caffyn wrote and published a hilarious account of the tour. Parr himself, prone to seasickness and terrified of icebergs, claimed to have found a cure for nervous sailors (gin and water) on the unpleasant outward journey, though he didn't have time to give it a proper trial until the return voyage. In New York, Julius Caesar got into a row with a local, and challenged him to a fist fight – but backed down when the man produced a gun.

The tour took little more than a month. The players were all professionals, and earned £90 each, more than the £50 they had initially been promised, and worth the best part of £10,000 today. There was every reason to do it all again, at least financially. The voyage home, though, proved a disincentive. "A fearful gale sprang up," wrote Caffyn. "Oh dear me! Jemmy Grundy declared we should never see land again, poor old Parr was nearly out of his mind, and Jackson dropped on his knees." One of the sailors was killed, and several of the cricketers refused ever to set foot on a ship again.

The catalyst for the next English tour was a company called Spiers & Pond, who ran several restaurants in Melbourne. Christopher Pond was an Englishman – one of many to have emigrated on the famous SS *Great Britain* – and keen to bring English attractions to Australia. He wrote to Charles Dickens, asking him to undertake a lecture tour for £10,000, but did not receive a reply. So William Spiers – a practical man with an eye for business – dispatched an employee, W. B. Mallam, to England, to search out Parr and ask him to bring a cricket team, for £150 a man. Parr, still bearing the mental scars of the Atlantic voyage (and unimpressed by the fee for a six-month trip), gave a curt refusal. So did most of the American tour party – but not all.

Caffyn, despite having been so traumatised by the Atlantic voyage that he told Lillywhite he "would not venture to leave England again under any circumstances, and if he did, he would forfeit £100", decided to go. So did Surrey's H. H. Stephenson, the first man to be awarded a hat for taking three wickets with successive deliveries, which he did at Sheffield in 1858. Stephenson, perhaps tempted by the offer of the captaincy, said he could persuade a number of his county team-mates. He was right. Mallam got his men, much to the irritation (and perhaps jealousy) of Parr.

The 1861-62 tour began and ended with matches in Melbourne and surrounding Victoria, with a month-long interlude in New South Wales and Tasmania. Once again, all the local opponents fielded oversized teams, but Stephenson's side were nowhere near as strong as Parr's. They were beaten by a combined New South Wales and Victoria XXII at Sydney, and also lost to Castlemaine towards the end of the trip.

Sydney was soon to gain a reputation for rowdy behaviour. The next winter, during a game between New South Wales and Victoria, home batsman Sidney Jones was given out in circumstances so contentious as to threaten future relations between the two states. In facing a delivery, he overbalanced, and steadied himself with his bat. The long-stop fielder returned the ball to the wicketkeeper, George Marshall, who whipped off the bails – and Marshall's appointed umpire, John Smith, raised his finger. The New South Wales captain strode out, saying his team would not continue unless Jones was called back. The umpires awarded Victoria the game, but the fracas did not end there.

> When the Melbourne men attempted to leave the ground, they were surrounded by a dense mob of excited ruffians, who were not satisfied with yelling and shrieking, but committed acts of personal violence upon several of the players. At length, however, under an escort of police, they retired. Marshall was mobbed and hustled in the evening by a crowd who followed him from his hotel. — *Bell's Life in Victoria*

The following day, tempers had cooled. Jones was reinstated, and the game resumed – albeit without Marshall or Smith, who refused to continue. Jones added eight to his score, and New South Wales went on to win. The controversy rumbled on, threatening to derail plans for a second English tour to Australia, two years after the first. The architect of this project, on the English side, was Parr. He was envious of the fame Stephenson had gained in Australia, and had been reassured by Caffyn that the sea trip, compared with the Atlantic, "was like taking a sail down the Thames". It had also become obvious that the financial rewards of a trip to Australia went far beyond the basic tour fee.

On 1 October, Parr's Twelve – a much stronger team than Stephenson's – met at Thomas Box's hostelry, by Leicester Square, to receive an advance of £50 (they each stood to make at least another £200 through advertising and benefit games). They then went to Lord's for photographs. Alongside Parr were six who had accompanied him across the Atlantic, and five undertaking their maiden voyage. For the first time, an amateur was among them: E. M. 'Teddy' Grace, the sporting sensation of the age, and perhaps the most famous cricketer to have yet lived. Several newspapers published pen portraits of the touring party.

THE TWELVE IN AUSTRALIA, 1863-64

George Parr b. Radcliffe-on-Trent, Nottinghamshire. Age: 37. Captain of Nottinghamshire. Tour to America, 1859-60. The stentorian 'Lion of the North' was once considered the greatest batsman since Fuller Pilch, and still maintains his reputation, but is not quite so active or fast a run-getter as formerly. He is occasionally struck by illness, which prevents him playing.

George Anderson b. Bedale, Yorkshire. Age: 37. Tour debutant. A most brilliant hitter, a fine field and a sure catch, he was originally brought before the public by the late veteran Clarke, whose bowling he used to punish much. A hearty eater – a great hand at pies and cheese cakes – but his appetite can be diminished by seasickness, from which he suffers terribly.

Julius Caesar b. Godalming, Surrey. Age: 33. Tour to America, 1859-60. A small man, and a nervous one, who hates sleeping by himself in any unfamiliar hotel. But as a plucky bat, and hard hitter, no one can excel him. He also has a very strong defence. He is busy at point, and every now and then he is asked to bowl.

Billy Caffyn b. Reigate, Surrey. Age: 35. Tour to America, 1859-60. Tour to Australia, 1861-62. He cuts and hits to square leg with great force. In the field he is a splendid cover or midwicket, and bowls accurate medium-pacers. He can play the cornet and the harp, and is fond of practical jokes, which have earned him the nickname 'Terrible Billy'. He is sometimes on the receiving end, though: his Surrey team-mates once placed a dead mouse in his best silk top hat. Caffyn is a favourite of the public – and of mosquitoes.

Bob Carpenter b. Cambridge, Cambridgeshire. Age: 32. Tour to America, 1859-60. As a batsman, quite at the top of the tree. His magnificent play is the admiration of all who witness it. A masterly defender, wonderful stroke-maker, and therefore a pretty sure run-getter. To the faster bowlers he advances down the pitch, and hits like a horse kicking. Slow bowlers find him impossible, but he nurses them for a run a ball, so as to keep them bowling.

Alfred Clarke b. Nottingham, Nottinghamshire. Age: 32. Tour debutant. William Mortlock had agreed to sign up for the tour, but changed his mind, and Parr was obliged to cast about for a twelfth player. He settled on the late William Clarke's son Alfred, who scored a half-century for Parr's Nottinghamshire side in 1862. He is by some distance the weakest cricketer of the group.

E. M. (Teddy) **Grace** b. Downend, Gloucestershire, and has not yet played county cricket. Age: 21. Tour debutant. Right-handed batsman, (mainly) slow bowler, occasional wicketkeeper. This gentleman is a thorough cricketer in every sense of the word. He is a first-rate bat, and has scored many hundreds. He is also an excellent bowler, usually slow but occasionally fast, and a good field. His play during 1863 fully sustained his reputation as the best gentleman player of the day: he averaged 40, but scandalised cricketing purists by routinely making cross-batted shots to leg.

Tom Hayward b. Chatteris, Cambridgeshire. Age: 28. Tour to America, 1859-60. The most naturally talented player of the Twelve, but with the most slender physical resources, being rather below medium height, extremely thin, and prone to poor health. He has a masterly defence, combined with the requisite hitting, and is a remarkably straight bowler of moderate pace. Hayward is also one of the best longstops about, possessing a very quick return to the wicketkeeper. When that man is Lockyer, many a batsman rues an attempted quick single.

John Jackson b. Bungay, Suffolk, but plays for Nottinghamshire. Age: 30. Tour to America, 1859-60. At over six feet high, 'Foghorn' is a relentlessly fast and accurate bowler. If he cannot bowl a man out, he will bump him out. Every now and then, if he is being hit, he will deliver a fast, high, full-pitch ball, aimed at the batsman's head, and follow it up with a look of undisguised fury.

Tom Lockyer b. Croydon, Surrey. Age: 30. Tour to America, 1859-60. He is still the wicketkeeper of the day, and a stumper absolutely without parallel. With the bat, he continually bothers the bowler and field with his pugnacious defence.

George Tarrant b. Cambridge, Cambridgeshire. Age: 24. Tour debutant. 'Tear 'em' Tarrant may not be a lovable character, but he is very fast, which makes him an indispensable asset of any team in which he plays. He alternates a bumper over head height with a toe-crushing yorker. When bowling with Jackson, he is a frightening prospect, and many a batsman of quality may be found backing anxiously to leg.

Cris Tinley b. Southwell, Nottinghamshire. Age: 32. Tour debutant. 'The Spider' is about the best of the underarm slow bowlers now playing, and may be second only to William Clarke, in any era. He delivers hip-high, and at a fair pace, giving the batsman little chance of coming down the pitch. He turns the ball so sharply, he is sometimes also referred to as 'The Corkscrew'.

The SS *Great Britain* embarked from Liverpool on 15 October – later than intended, because the ship was being fitted with larger boilers. The Twelve had been presented with 1,000 cigars by a Manchester businessman named Whittaker, "as a solace during their 16,000 miles voyage, and that they may frequently think of him," according to the *Sporting Gazette*.

Parr's men were accommodated in saloon class, with about seventy other passengers. Three of the cricketers kept an account of the journey. One was Billy Caffyn, who had kept up his writing since the trip to America. Teddy Grace, being a gentleman, kept a private diary, and George Anderson was induced to put pen to paper by a fee from the *Sporting Gazette*. Neither had made such a journey before, and only one found his sea-legs.

OCTOBER

14th [TG] Saw my bunk fellow-passenger board before me, so he had first choice, and I am below him, but I think I shall find I have the best end of the stick. [GA] Went on board. Sick for the first week.

15th [BC] I have been valeting Anderson while he is sick: cutting his hair, shampooing him, etc. [TG] I began to feel very queer.

17th [TG] Much better. Jumping competition on deck: at standing long-jump I jumped farthest, and also licked them at running long-jump. Caffyn started playing the cornet. Anderson very bad in bed since starting. Tarrant also unwell.

19th [GA] With a little help got on deck. [TG] For the first time, played at bull-board.

20th [TG] Had a turn at quoits.

23rd [TG] I can now lick all the rest at quoits and bull-board. [BC] We had some great fun when we started 'cock-fighting'. Two opponents had a stick passed at the back of their knee joints, and held it there with their arms. While in this position each had to try to knock the other over.

24th [GA] Managed to play a game of bull-board on deck. Saw the first whale. [TG] A passenger, while pretending to box with Carpenter, lost his bowler hat overboard. Regret to record, a little child, five years of age, died of dysentery this evening.

25th [TG] Child buried in the deep at 2.30am.

29th [GA] Meeting in the saloon for setting up a judge and jury for the amusement of the passengers.

30th [TG] Caesar got the gout rather severely.

31st [GA] First trial: case of attempted poisoning! Prisoner, Mr. Maguire, acquitted, and prosecutor, Mr. Bright, fined bottle of champagne.

NOVEMBER

1st [GA] Still prone to lengthy bouts of sickness, but when well, bull-board and dancing on the deck.

3rd [TG] Crossed the Line at 6pm. [BC] A lighted tar-barrel was thrown overboard. This we could see after we had left it miles behind, and it produced a grand effect in the darkness of the night.

4th [TG] A passenger named Burchett has a propensity to walk very fast up and down the deck, so we got up a match, Burchett v Tarrant, to walk ten times up and down the saloon. Burchett 2 min 58 secs, Tarrant 2 min 25 secs. Tarrant clever winner.

9th [GA] Captain Gray got a severe fall on deck after dark and injured himself much about the face. The passengers all sorry, he being a favourite with all. [BC] Capt. Gray is a remarkably nice man, and has endeared himself to all by his many acts of kindness.

10th [GA] Concert of vocal and instrumental music by the second class passengers on deck. As good as might be expected.

14th [GA] Played a little at cricket, but very shaky. Lockyer fishing for an albatross, but without success. [TG] Caffyn played a solo on the cornet very fairly.

18th [TG] Tarrant got tooth ache. Cured him by pulling the tooth out, did so luckily at first pull, but required all my strength, so tremendously tight was it in.

19th [TG] Tarrant enjoyed rare fun fishing for birds, using about 200 yards of line, baited with a piece of pork.

21st [TG] A concert. Piano excruciatingly out of tune, but Anderson sang 'God Bless the Prince of Wales' very well.

23rd [GA] Now playing whist at nights.

25th [GA] A good deal of betting on the distance run. [TG] Bet odds we do not do 350 miles today. Won, but very close shave.

By November, New Zealand's *Lyttelton Times* giddily reported that there was a chance that the Twelve might come to play there. A special delegation was sent to negotiate with the Australians, only to find them still at loggerheads. Joseph Clayton, the secretary of New South Wales Cricket Club, was exchanging heated letters with W. C. Biddle, his opposite number in Melbourne. "We cannot at present consent to enter into any negotiations," wrote Clayton, "without something being done on the part of your committee to remove the unpleasantness … our committee feel something is due to their representatives, who have been so vilely slandered". Biddle, for his part, felt the dispute "should be allowed to drop", but the Sydney men stuck to their guns. *Bell's Life* was at a loss to understand why. "The last trip of the English cricketers to Sydney was pre-eminently successful, and the Sydney people have any amount of pluck in such speculations as this," they wrote. "We do not think they will allow such a magnificent team to leave Australia without having a taste of their quality."

New South Wales's stance may, at least in part, have been due to the fact that George Marshall – the Melbourne wicketkeeper whom they felt had wronged them – was taking care of the tour arrangements on Parr's behalf. Marshall was a wealthy timber merchant from Surrey, well placed to make business deals. And his arrangements, in Victoria at least, were well advanced. A new grandstand, with seating for 5,000, was nearing completion at the old police paddock in Yarra Park, one day to become the gargantuan Melbourne Cricket Ground. As in 1861-62, fixtures were firmed up in Bendigo, Ballarat, Castlemaine and Geelong – Beechworth would miss out this time – and matches were added at Ararat and Maryborough. Tasmania once again asked to host games, as did Adelaide. Marshall demanded payment of £2,000 and all expenses paid. The general view was that South Australia would find the money, Parr's men would visit Adelaide, and New South Wales would be off the programme entirely.

Into this melee stepped the New Zealanders, with an offer of £3,500, plus all travelling and hotel expenses, for a three-week visit from the English. Neither South Australia nor Tasmania could compete with that kind of money. Three weeks weren't quite enough to fill the gap created by the absence of a visit to New South Wales, so a return-trip stopover in Calcutta was mooted.

None of these developments was known back in England. The mail ship left Australia on the 26th day of each month, and arrived around the 12th of the next month but one – a journey of about six and a half weeks. November's negotiations would not be public in Britain until the new year, by which time apparently disastrous tidings had arrived.

DECEMBER

1st [TG] Was to have Ethiopian Serenaders this evening, but did not, because gentlemen declined to 'blacken their beards'.

3rd [TG] Have an ugly gathering on the first finger of my left hand – bad look-out for my batting.

4th [TG] My finger worse.

6th [TG] Had finger lanced.

9th [GA] Concert by saloon passengers in evening, which gave great satisfaction. I sang four times.

12th [TG] Finger worse today, so had it lanced to the bone, and trust it will be all right in time for play.

13th [GA] The ninth Sunday on board. I could not get to service – sick again, like the rest of the weakly ones. [BC] I never saw anyone suffer so much from seasickness as Anderson. The malady always returned when the ocean became at all rough. He was reduced to quite a skeleton.

15th [GA] Very heavy gale with haze and a rough sea. Felt nervous and queer as we were not far from land, and consequently in some danger.

On 30 December, the news came to England that the *Great Britain*, bound from London for the Antipodes, had been wrecked off Cape Verde; the crew and passengers had all been saved, but were stranded on the island of Santiago. Three days later, enquiries by the panic-stricken press established that there were two ships of the same name – and it was a clipper, not a steamer, that had foundered. The SS *Great Britain*, with the English cricketers aboard, was safe.

In fact, the ship had entered Port Phillip Bay on 16 December (this reassuring information would not reach Britain until mid-February). Marshall was the first to meet the Twelve, who disembarked the following day, and were conveyed through immense crowds to Marshall's Hotel. They had two weeks to settle in, practise and attend receptions before their first game, scheduled for New Year's Day. Grace left off his diary on arrival, but Anderson was contractually bound to continue. His entries were a little lacking in colour.

> **18th** Looking around town. Could almost fancy myself in England.
>
> **19th** Several Yorkshire people called. Went to Brighton for practice.
>
> **20th** Photographs.
>
> **21st** Going about town trying to make out people.
>
> **22nd** Went to Brighton to practise.
>
> **23rd** Writing letter home.
>
> **24th** Writing and posting letters, then went to St Kilda.
>
> **25th** Christmas Day. At home till after dinner.
>
> **26th** Picnic at Sunbury.
>
> **27th** At Mr. Kirk's in the morning, then at Brighton.
>
> **28th** Watched Melbourne play Sydney at cricket.
>
> **29th** At practice on the Melbourne ground.
>
> **30th** Further practice, then dined with the Mayor.
>
> **31st** Further practice.

It may not make for thrilling reading, but Anderson's diary for the second half of December raises two points. The first is that there was a good deal more acclimatisation and practice than an England team touring Australia would bother with in the 21st century. The second is that relations between the Melbourne and New South Wales clubs appeared to be thawing, since they were now playing each other once more. It probably helped that Smith was not umpiring, Marshall was too busy to play, and Jones was inarguably out, caught for five. Melbourne lost again.

JANUARY

Nineteenth-century English winters were unusually cold. The Northern Hemisphere was still in a frigid spell known as the Little Ice Age, and the Thames often froze – though the 1831 demolition of London Bridge, allowing the current to flow more freely, had put an end to the tradition of frost fairs on the river.

Ponds iced over so thickly that skating was the most popular winter pastime in the country. The smooth surfaces were perfect for cricket, and a freeze during the first three weeks of January 1864 brought forth a profusion of games. The *Sheffield Daily Telegraph* reported that the local skating club was actually scheduling fixtures. Mr. Ainley's XI beat Mr. Birtles's XI by 40 runs to 28 at Little London Dam, while a six-a-side game between Mr. Tasker's team and Mr. Gillott's team saw prodigious scoring, "as the ball, once struck, found no obstruction before reaching the banks".

Games, with scores, were reported as far away as John O'Groats. In Sussex, a match was played between a team on skates and a team on foot, but night fell before a result could be obtained. Sudden fog ended a match in Shropshire.

Cricket and ice were, unsurprisingly, uneasy bedfellows. An account in the *Ulverston Mirror and Furness Reflector*, in Cumberland, explained why: "The difficulty of stopping was, of course, fully appreciated, and the nervous grasping of each other by two or more individuals – to preserve their equilibrium when a faux pas by one might have involved the spilling of several – made it apparent that cricket in skates is a matter of no small moment."

During the last deep freeze, in 1860-61, at least 160 people had been rescued from the ice. In 1864, the Royal Humane Society in London tried to warn people off, then set up first-aid posts and hot baths at any sizeable pond. Three years later, in Regent's Park, hundreds were flung into the water when the ice broke. Many floundered in their heavy winter clothing, and two wicker boats were launched in a forlorn attempt at rescue. Forty people died. The ice-cricketers of 1864 were fortunate to face no greater mishap than a bit of rough and tumble.

In Melbourne, the weather was sweltering. The grand stand was completed – and filled – by the time the English took the field on New Year's Day. The city fancied itself a well-to-do place, just as it imagined Sydney a redneck one, and the crowds wore their Sunday best, showing "the utmost decorum and order", according to the *Morning Star.* Marshall selected the Victoria team, which included Tom Wills, an ex-captain of the Rugby School team, and a pioneer of Australian rules football. He travelled 1,800 miles from north Queensland, but arrived only on the last day; Marshall allowed him to join in as a substitute fielder.

At Melbourne, January 1, 2, 4, 5. **Drawn. ‡Victoria XXII 146** (W. H. Greaves 34; J. Jackson 6-48, R. C. Tinley 11-53) **and 143** (J. Jackson 4-18, R. C. Tinley 8-63, G. Tarrant 7-37); **England 176** (T. Hayward 61, R. P. Carpenter 59; S. Cosstick 4-62, J. M. Bryant 6-43) **and 105-4** (W. Caffyn 37*). *Clarke umpired.*

The hosts won the toss, and the English took the field wearing white hats, and white flannel shirts with a red spot. Marshall faced the first ball of the tour, bowled by Jackson, in front of about 14,000 spectators. The Victorians had a tricky time negotiating Tinley's slows, but while he earned 19 wickets, they made some headway, passing 140 in both innings (William Greaves's first-day 34 was the highest score made by any Australian during the tour). In between, the English made 176, the bulk coming in a five-hour stand of 125 between Hayward and Carpenter – no mean feat with 20 outfielders. They came within nine of a target of 114, but ran out of time.

The English newspapers considered this a moral victory, not least on account of what they saw as time-wasting by the home players. According to Anderson, the Victorians countered the heat by repeatedly stopping for brandy. "The players went to the tents to 'liquor up', as they term it here. The climate is certainly very warm, and may induce thirst – but not such an unquenchable

A patient at the Glasgow Lunatic Asylum, fit to be discharged, could not be persuaded to leave for several months. He was much attached to the institution, and took interest in the amusements, being one of the best cricketers in the Asylum. Matches were a source of recreation among the patients, and contributed to their recovery. — *Glasgow Herald*, 15 January

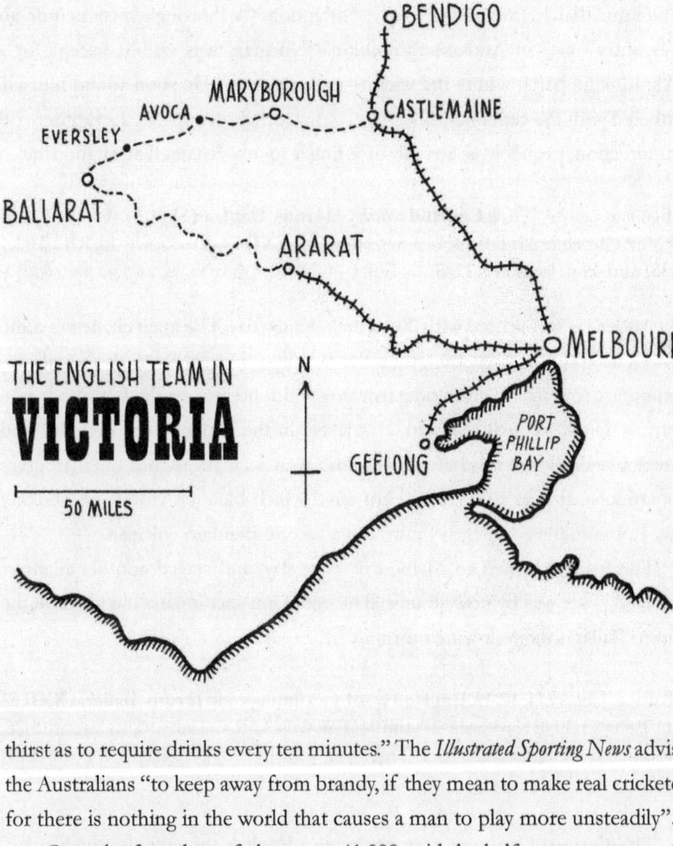

thirst as to require drinks every ten minutes." The *Illustrated Sporting News* advised the Australians "to keep away from brandy, if they mean to make real cricketers, for there is nothing in the world that causes a man to play more unsteadily".

Over the four days of the game, 41,000 paid the half-crown entrance fee, bringing in more than £5,000. The tour had largely paid for itself within a week. One spectator, who had played at St John's Wood as a boy, walked 100 miles from his house to the ground, just to see an English cricket team once more.

On the evening of 6 January, the Twelve – accompanied by Marshall and Wills – took the train to Bendigo, a gold-mining town just under a hundred miles to the North. The countryside around was parched, and the heat broiling; Lockyer observed several bushfires on the journey. The pitch for the three-day game immediately excited the tourists' attention. "A thorough specimen of an up-country one," in Anderson's opinion. "No grass was visible, except for a sickly-looking patch where the wickets were pitched." He soon found himself lumbered with the captaincy, since Parr was struck by erysipelas, a streptococcal skin infection, probably as a result of a finger injury sustained at Melbourne.

At Bendigo, January 7, 8, 9. **England won by 144 runs. England 85** (T. W. Wills 6-35) **and 178** (R. P. Carpenter 33; T. W. Wills 3-57); **‡Bendigo XXII 74** (J. Jackson 6-10, R. C. Tinley 13-35) **and 45** (J. Jackson 7-12, R. C. Tinley 14-22). *Parr, being unwell, umpired sporadically.*

Anderson top-scored with 26 on the opening day. The main challenge came from Wills, recruited to strengthen the Bendigo team, who took six wickets, mixing fast roundarm with underarm slows. But he made a duck in the locals' reply, as Tinley – on his way to 27 wickets in the match – ensured England gained a lead. By the third afternoon, they were well ahead, but their progress was arduous, thanks to a strong, hot wind which blew up clouds of choking dust. It was followed by heavy rain, and a second Bendigo collapse.

The team returned to Melbourne next day, and stayed another night at Marshall's. Parr was by now so unwell he could not accompany the team on the train to Ballarat the following morning.

At Ballarat, January 11, 12, 13. **England won by an innings and 12 runs. Ballarat XXII 82** (R. C. Tinley 13-30, T. Hayward 7-27) **and 94** (T. W. Wills 32; R. C. Tinley 10, T. Hayward 5-26, J. Jackson 3-8); **‡England 188** (G. F. Tarrant 32, W. Caffyn 39, J. Caesar 40, T. Lockyer 31; T. W. Wills 4-60, J. M. Bryant 4-40). *Parr remained in Melbourne.*

The Eastern Oval was very pretty, and English thought the pitch vastly better than at Bendigo, though the *Melbourne Herald* was critical: "Beyond the wickets, the ground was very rough, making brilliant fielding at a distance an impossibility. This state of the ground is not from any neglect on the part of the Ballarat Club, but owing to the overflows of sludge which periodically occur."

Wills again played for the local team, and it was just as well he did: his four wickets stopped England running away with the game, and his 32 saved face in Ballarat's innings defeat. Tinley took his wicket tally to 69 in three games, but

Carpenter suffered a thumb injury while batting. The culprit was Jerry Bryant, a Melbourne hotelier who had fleetingly played for Surrey before emigrating in the 1850s, and was now emerging as Australia's main strike bowler (and most proficient groundsman).

The match ended early on the third day, so an impromptu game was organised: Grace and Tarrant against eight Australians. Bryant and Wills took a wicket each, but a target of 21 proved too great; neither scored a run.

After two nights' cosy accommodation at the Royal Hotel – which came with free admission to the neighbouring theatre – the English returned to discomfort with a jarring overnight coach journey to Ararat. The 60 miles of bumpy track took them ten hours, and Lockyer was dismayed that several lost the rims to their hats. They arrived at their hotel at half past nine, hoping for a bath and a lie down, but were shown to two dormitories, with nine beds for the 12 of them. By the time they had found new quarters, it was time for the match.

At Ararat, January 14, 15. **England won by an innings and 68 runs. ‡England 137** (R. P. Carpenter 36; T. W. Wills 6-57, F. Lowe 3-42); **Ararat XXII 35** (R. C. Tinley 14-22, J. Jackson 7-11) **and 34** (R. C. Tinley 12-23, E. M. Grace 7-4). *Parr was in Melbourne, and Hayward was ill, so Marshall played for England.*

"There was no grass at all on the wicket, and the reflection of the bright sun from it was most distressing to the eyes." So wrote Anderson, who continued to lead the team. Carpenter's thumb was better, but Hayward had fallen ill, so Marshall stepped in, and hit a respectable 14, before becoming one of six victims

Thomas Abbott was sued by George Farmery for £2 for damage to his person (specifically his nose) in Knaresborough. Farmery: Abbott threatened to spoil my nose, and then struck me several times. Judge: And you value your nose at £2 (laughter). Abbott: I hit him once only. Farmery: I could not eat or sleep for three days. Abbott: He was playing cricket that evening, and on the organ next day. Judge: He says you damaged his organ (laughter). Mr Farmery, did you go about with your nose in a sling? Farmery: Yes, he hit me very hard. Judge: A shilling plaster is quite large enough for your nose (roars of laughter). Judgement for the defendant. — *Tadcaster Post*, 28 January for Wills. Tinley again bamboozled the opposition, none of whom scored more than eight. When Ararat followed on, Grace had his first bowl of the tour, and claimed seven for four in 23 (four-ball) overs; Lockyer made seven stumpings.

The contest ought to have lasted three days, but was over in two. A big crowd was expected on the final day, a Saturday, so Tarrant agreed to step into the limelight, single-handedly taking on an Ararat XI. He dismissed them all for a total of four, but found it hard to thread the ball into the gaps, and was caught for four from the 73rd delivery he faced. The one-against-eleven tie caused a sensation. Everyone wanted a piece of Tarrant. "A man has only to achieve some extraordinary success and it is astonishing how those who have previously regarded him with indifference claim relationship," wrote *Sporting Life*. "Tarrant has always been regarded as a Cambridgeshire man, and played for that county, but Surrey have long asserted that Tarrant was born there. Now this great cricketer has played and tied a whole eleven in Australia, Hampshire has also laid claim to the honour of having been his birthplace." The editor of the *Ararat Advertiser*, noting that the English players' eyes were all blue, concluded that this must be the attribute that bestowed cricketing ability.

The next the journey was another 60-mile boneshaker to Maryborough, but the tourists decided to split it over two days, spending a night at Eversley. There they were hosted by a Yorkshireman named Little, who arranged shooting and fishing parties. Lockyer particularly relished "possuming by moonlight", and his bloodlust was further satisfied in the morning: "We had the pleasure of seeing a black snake that had just been killed by an Australian youth. It measured about 6ft 6in, and was about as thick as one's arm". Anderson savoured the experience rather less, shrieking that he had been bitten by a snake. It turned out to be a long black stick.

James Anderson, a young man, was charged with being drunk and disorderly on Saturday morning, laid upon his back in the street, and calling to people passing. At the Petty Sessions in Accrington, Mr. Carswell said Anderson had been to the cricketers' ball, and had taken "a drop too much". The defendant was told to pay expenses. — *Preston Chronicle*, 30 January

The English enjoyed an enormous lunch in Avoca, and were a few miles from Maryborough when half the town, wild with excitement, rode out to meet them. The evening entertainment was provided by Christy's Minstrels, a blackface troupe from New York. Lockyer met a parrot who could say almost anything, and organised a whip-round for £50, but the owner would not sell.

At Maryborough, January 19, 20, 21. **England won by an innings and 77 runs.** **‡Maryborough XXII 72** (T. Hayward 9-41, R. C. Tinley 11-24) **and 74** (R. C. Tinley 11-48; J. Jackson 6-5); **England 223** (E. M. Grace 44, T. Hayward 30, W. Caffyn 32, T. Lockyer 30). *Parr was still in Melbourne.*

Maryborough brought more dust, a third successive innings victory. Even though a new pitch was used for every innings, a total absence of grass meant the dust was six inches deep around the wickets. The slow bowlers, on both sides, loved it. Tinley passed the 100-wicket mark on the first afternoon, and Wills claimed another five for the locals.

Once again, the contest finished early on the third day and, after a luncheon in their honour, the Twelve took a late coach ride to Castlemaine, where they spent the evening. They expended their surplus energy with foot races, Grace easily defeating Tarrant in a 100-yard sprint. From Castlemaine, they returned by train to Melbourne, where they met the much-recovered Parr. While they awaited the steamer *Alhambra*, their transport to New Zealand, they wrote letters home. The *Alhambra* departed on 25 January, and the mail ship the following day; news of the matches in Victoria reached London on 12 March.

Anderson, inevitably, had a terrible time during the six-day voyage across the Tasman. So bad was his vertigo, he fell out of his bunk, grazing his leg, injuring his shoulder, and knocking a large basin onto the head of Caffyn, below him. Caffyn was badly cut, and wore sticking-plasters in the sign of a cross for several days. His team-mates took to calling him 'The Warrior' and, according to the *Sporting Gazette*, "his opinion of sea voyages in general, and of New Zealand in particular, was given with more force than elegance of phraseology". Caffyn bore the scar for the rest of his life.

FEBRUARY

For fifteen years, there had been only one cricket annual: Fred Lillywhite's *Guide to Cricketers*. By the end of 1863, its 17 editions had sold over 120,000 copies, and it was now published twice a year. But Lillywhite's monopoly was about to be broken, by not one rival, but two.

The first to make a move were A. H. Baily & Co. in London, publishers of *Baily's Monthly Magazine of Sports and Pastimes* and *Baily's Turf Guide and Racing Register*. Their new initiative, the *Cricket Chronicle for 1863*, was first advertised in the *Evening Standard* on 15 December, and was immediately available, priced 2s 6d. Four days after Baily's advertisement, the *Sporting Gazette* and *Bell's Life* announced that the first edition of John Wisden's *Cricketer's Almanack* would shortly be published. About Lillywhite's *Guide*, there was nothing.

On 9 January, *Sporting Life* published a damning review of Baily's *Chronicle*. The matches were not in a chronological order, nor a logical one, and specific fixtures could only be found by consulting the index; county games were considered less important than private school matches; the book was "crowded with a vast number of insignificant scores … which no eyes except those of the individuals whose performances they record will ever care to rest upon".

At the end of the month, the *Sporting Gazette* was more generous: "The book is certainly not a beauty, but if not very ornamental it will be found decidedly useful. Nothing has come amiss to the gallant compiler: from an MCC match to a One Arm v One Leg affair, there are scores of no fewer than 746 matches played last season, filling 513 pages."

On 8 February, Wisden published his *Almanack*, for 1s 1d, including postage. This price undercut not only Baily, but also Lillywhite, who charged 1s 7d. *Sporting Life* reviewed the *Almanack* two days before publication.

> The work is published by the well-known cricket outfitters John Wisden and Co. at the charge of one shilling, under the title of the "Cricketer's Almanack", and although it falls short of our ideas of what a cricketer's almanack ought to be, it will be found extremely useful for reference, as it contains a calendar, in which are registered the births of most of the past and present cricket celebrities … At page 13, we have the laws

> of the game, and at page 17 the dates of the first appearances of great players at Lord's Ground, commencing with the year 1787, and ending with the season 1863. At page 27, we have a record of some extraordinary matches, which is followed by the full scores of the various matches between the Gentlemen and Players from its first institution in 1806, but without comment, the author observing "that the cricketer is left to form his own opinion with regard to the merits of the men". Next comes a similar register of the matches between the Two Elevens. Pages 98 to 102 present us with something that is entirely foreign to the subject, which we should think the "Cricketer's Almanack" would be quite as well without: lists of the Derby, Oaks and St. Leger winners. The more kindred exercises of knur and spell, bowls, and quoits are then treated of. A table of the University Rowing Matches follows, and a miscellaneous chapter or two extend the book to 112 pages. As a first effort, this little work of Wisden and Co. deserves commendation, and will doubtless be appreciated by cricketers.

Wisden had plenty of help producing the first *Almanack*. W. H. Knight, a cricket correspondent with *The Times*, wrote much of the text, and W. H. Crockford of Blackheath collated and printed the pages. There had to be a multiple of 16, for printing reasons, and the *Sporting Life* reviewer clearly realised that there had been trouble in reaching 112. Francis Cary Elwes, who regularly made up a shooting trio with Wisden and Parr, had helped fill the void. From his journal of rowing and racing events, he contributed a list of Boat Race winners, and may have been the source, or the inspiration, for all manner of irrelevant fillers.

> Page 26 "The graces of the modern tea-table were quite unknown to the country folk, although that favourite beverage, brought by the Dutch to Europe, was introduced to England by Lords Arlington and Ossory in 1666."
>
> *and* The nobility of England, and the House of Lords.
>
> Page 103 Key dates in the history of China.
>
> Page 109 List of the principal British Societies.
>
> Page 110 Definition of a Mayor.
>
> Page 111 List of British canals; history of clocks; history of coinage.
>
> Page 112 Dates of the Crusades and Wars of the Roses; incredulous account of the trial of King Charles I ["Where were the Peers?"]; description of the breaking of a massive brass bell at Woolwich in 1861.

The two "extraordinary matches" featured in the *Almanack* were an 1838 game in which all 32 players were more than 60 years old, and the 2nd Royal Surrey Militia being all out for nought in 1855.

Other than printing the Laws of Cricket in full, Wisden had almost no overlap with Lillywhite. The *Almanack* did not include a review of the 1863 season, nor any match reports, and tried to make a virtue of that: "a great many of our readers are at least equal, if not superior, to ourselves in arriving at the right judgment of play." Lillywhite and Baily had no such scruples. Neither did the newspapers – nor even Cary Elwes, who wrote his own match reports in his journal. A review in *The Era* decided the Almanack's main selling points were the full scores of all the matches between the Gentlemen and Players, and between the Two Elevens. It felt the quoits section was "touch-and-go", and the "paper, type and general get-up of the book" unexceptional. Somewhat pointedly, *The Era* then called Lillywhite's *Guide* an "old favourite" and said it would be available at the end of February. The review then remarked upon the number of cricket almanacks now available: "One of them must have a bad innings, we think." Prophetic words, as it turned out.

Lillywhite was, by now, struggling with his workload. His 1864 *Guide* did not appear at the end of February; it was not even advertised until March, when he claimed it was "the only cricketing guide published" and insisted it would be ready "about the first week of April". Another advert, in April, announced a further postponement, until May. By then, Wisden's book had been available for three months, and Baily's for nearly five. Realising his predicament, Lillywhite reduced the Guide from 1s 7d to a shilling. "It will contain remarks on all the professionals and gentlemen in England," he said.

Bell's Life, for which Lillywhite was cricket correspondent, lavished praise on the 1864 edition: "The synopsis of all good cricket past is there for those

> Mr. Holman, secretary of the Chalcot Cricket Club, Hampstead, sued Mr. Hodges, a civil engineer, for £5 9s, being five years' subscription to the club. Mr. Hodges admitted that he had played cricket for Chalcot, but withdrew after the second year, and considered his liability was at an end. His Honour made an order for £3 3s. — *Sporting Life*, 3 February

who wish to fight their battles o'er again and, for the Tyro who handles his bat for the first time this season, there are well-tried maxims and precepts for enabling him to rise to the highest step on the ladder." The *Sporting Gazette* wrote: "the new original matter is led off by a two-page review of the season, which review is like the writer – a very short and smart affair. The comments on the big matches of 1864 are quite in the 'Lilly' style – neat, quaint, and generally just – albeit we perceive, in page 23, he could not resist the pleasure of giving the United Eleven a poke in the ribs."

It was the slightest of pokes, merely suggesting that Wisden had missed a trick by organising the United Eleven's fixture with MCC when all his best players had a game with Surrey. But considerably worse pokes were to come. From a critic's or cricketer's perspective, Lillywhite had won 1864's battle of the almanacks. His loose tongue, however, would soon cost him the war.

~~

If the English Twelve experienced culture shock on arrival in New Zealand, they hid it well. After landing at Port Chalmers, the main port of Dunedin, they decided to go shooting, but stumbled upon a Māori settlement. "We were encircled by 60 or 70 of them, and were introduced to their king, a fine-looking old man," recalled Lockyer. The *Sporting Gazette* wrote: "The men were half-dressed like ordinary mortals, and the women – listen, ye Victorian belles! – in many instances wore crinoline, but never stockings or shoes. The Queen, who is tattooed all over, smokes a short pipe, and has a decided penchant for champagne, took a strong fancy for Parr's travelling rug, which was a very smart one. On his presenting her with it, she formally installed him as king of the tribe."

The ever-nervous Parr found it all a bit much. His coronation ceremony required him to kiss every woman in the community, and whenever his team-mates stepped away, he would hiss: "Don't leave me, for goodness sake!" The English slept at their anchorage that night, and for once Parr was relieved to be on board ship.

Next morning, 1 February, a six-horse coach – driven by a local character described only as 'Cabbage Tree Ned' – carried the Twelve along the precipitous, windswept track to Dunedin. "Large trees had been blown down across the road," wrote Lockyer. "There was no fence, and at certain points a perpendicular descent of many hundreds of feet. Many times our coach wheels could not have been more than three inches off a fall." The dangers did not come to an end when they reached town: the newspaper office next to their hotel caught fire.

At Dunedin, February 2, 3, 4. **England won by nine wickets. Otago XXII 71** (T. Hayward 15-34, J. Jackson 5-22) **and 83** (T. Hayward 9-36, J. Jackson 6-20, R. C. Tinley 4-20); **‡England 99** (J. Redfearn 4-6, F. MacDonald 3-48, J. Mace 3-40) **and 58-1.** *Anderson was sick, and Wills umpired.*

Though the streets were crammed with well-wishers, the ground was by no means full, the previous day's gales having stripped the roof off the stand. The admission fee was reduced from a half-crown to a shilling, but to little effect. Anderson, too seasick to participate, described the pitch as "the very worst that cricket was ever played upon" and, on winning the toss, Parr decided not to risk batting first. All the local batsmen could think about was escaping injury, and Hayward helped himself to 15 wickets on the first day. That evening, during

At a meeting of the Godalming Institute, the Rev. T. Davis brought a resolution that the *Bell's Life* newspaper be removed from the reading room table, on these grounds: first, that the principal events were reported in other papers; second, that those who wished to read it could do so at other places than the reading room of the Institute; third, that it was decidedly immoral. Mr. Stedman protested against any dictation by any member as to what the other members should read. Mr. Dashper thought the reading room ought to have something to suit the tastes of all, and though he very seldom looked at it himself, he would not vote to prevent other persons from reading it. Mr H. Roker thought people could learn evil from other papers besides *Bell's Life* if they were so inclined. He read *Bell's Life* for the cricket matches, and he did not think his morals were corrupted by reading it. Five voted in favour of Reverend Davis's proposition and 20 against. — *Bell's Life*, 20 February dinner, another building caught fire, opposite the hotel. Lockyer watched, fascinated. "It raged all night with unabated fury, and its progress was arrested only by having the houses in the immediate vicinity pulled down ere the flames could reach them. The street flowed with beer, which had been rolled out of the stores, the heads of the casks being broken in by stones, or rather by the mob."

England chiselled out a lead of 28, and a fresh pitch, perpendicular to the first, was prepared for the third day. It was not much better, and England won by an innings. Despite their dislike of the conditions, they agreed to a second game. Wills, brought along as umpire, captained the locals this time.

At Dunedin, February 4, 5. Drawn. ‡**Canterbury and Otago XXII 91** (R. C. Tinley 14 wickets) **and 66** (R. C. Tinley 13 wickets); **England 73** (E. M. Grace 42). *Anderson umpired.*

Tinley, who had only a brief, belated bowl in the first contest, now cashed in, claiming 27 wickets. Grace top-scored with an unusually fluky 42, surviving a plumb lbw shout and four catching chances. England gave up a first innings lead, but time ran out before they could have a crack at a target of 85. Then, much to Anderson's despair, came another sea trip: 200 miles up the coast to Christchurch.

They arrived on 6 February, and Lockyer observed yet more misadventure. "We anchored in the beautiful port of Lyttelton, where a public reception would have been accorded us, but we did not get ashore until midnight: one of the boatmen lost an oar, and the boat beginning to drift with the tide, some of our men, having the fear of sharks in them, shouted most lustily for aid."

The following day, a Sunday, Caesar went for a ride along the cliffs, but his horse bolted and he nearly fell to his death. Next morning, he was so traumatised he refused to board the coach over the bluffs towards Christchurch, insisting on travelling by foot. A train was to take the Twelve from Heathcote into town, but had to wait for Caesar, and the match at Hagley Park started several hours late.

At Christchurch, February 8, 9, 10. **England won by an innings and two runs. Canterbury XXII 30** (J. Jackson 6-11, R. C. Tinley 13-18) **and 105** (J. Jackson 3-20, R. C. Tinley 12-68, T. Hayward 3-10); ‡**England 137** (T. W. Wills 6-55). *Caesar was evidently still too shaken to play.*

The delay mattered little. Though Wills played for Christchurch, he was run out for four, and the entire innings was completed in a couple of hours on the first afternoon. The English had to bat before the close, and Grace's stumps were scattered by Wills's first delivery. A new pitch was cut next morning – a routine procedure on underprepared cricket grounds – and the tourists built up 137, eight batsmen reaching double figures, but none passing 23. Tinley began scything through the locals again, but eventually met resistance, in the form of Augustus Eatwell Tennant, who made 28 on the third day. The match still ended ahead of time, and an exhibition game had to be pulled together. And it was quite a contest, since it was the first time on the tour that eleven played eleven.

At Christchurch, February 10, 11. **Parr's XI won by seven runs. Parr's XI 64** (E. M. Grace 5 wickets, T. W. Wills 3 wickets) **and 89** (A. E. Tennant 33; E. M. Grace 5 wickets, T. W. Wills 3 wickets); **Anderson's XI 71** (W. Caffyn 3 wickets, T. Hayward 6 wickets) **and 75** (W. Caffyn 4 wickets, T. Hayward 6 wickets). *Toss not known.*

Parr had Caffyn, Clarke, Hayward, Tarrant and Tinley, plus Tennant; Anderson had Caesar, Carpenter, Grace, Jackson and Locker, plus Wills. Grace put on a virtuoso performance, hitting the two highest scores of the game, and claiming five wickets in each innings – but still ended up on the losing side. Parr's XI completed victory without the services of Tinley, who fell ill on the second day.

On the way back to the ship, all of the Twelve shared Caesar's preference for walking from Heathcote to Lyttelton, preferring not to risk a fatal fall. They left on the same steamer that had brought them, and returned to Dunedin on the evening of 14 February. Next day, a match was arranged, pitting the best Otago XI against Grace and Tarrant, with Caffyn fielding. The English pair managed only eight between them: the weather was so cold that Grace batted with his waistcoat on, and the pitch so rough that one delivery bounced up and broke his wristwatch, and another hit his pocket and smashed his pencil case (it says much for Grace's attitude towards the game that he declined to leave his pencils in the pavilion). Tarrant single-handedly dismissed the locals for seven, bowling ten and taking a return catch off the eleventh.

At Dunedin, February 16, 17, 18. **England won by an innings and 51 runs. England 198** (W. Caffyn 43, T. Hayward 40; F. MacDonald 4-40, J. Redfearn 4-40); **Otago XXII 98** (R. C. Tinley 8-64, J. Jackson 10-21) **and 49** (R. C. Tinley 11 wickets; J. Jackson 7 wickets). *Parr did not play. Toss not known.*

The final match in New Zealand was a repeat fixture against Otago. Though the locals they were bolstered by the inclusion of Willis, who captained (and top-scored, with 20 in the second innings), they lost even more heavily this time. England only had to bat once. When the game was over, they stuck around to engage each other in various races, partly for the entertainment of the day's spectators, but mainly to settle bets they had accrued. Grace lost his three head-to-heads, but won a ball-throwing contest, with a distance of 101 yards (later in the tour, he hurt his arm throwing 120 yards in competition with an Aboriginal spear-thrower). Before leaving the ground, each of the Twelve planted a memorial tree.

The mail had departed during the last Dunedin game, and would regale those back home with the Englishmen's exploits in New Zealand. When they embarked on another eight-day voyage across the Tasman Sea, they were still unbeaten – but the tour was only halfway through.

MARCH

Cricket had been seen in India since the early eighteenth century: wherever there was English trade, there was cricket. The crews of trading ships exercised by playing on deck, and there is an early mention of a game – on land, and involving locals – in Bombay in 1784. But Calcutta appears to have been the birthplace of properly organised cricket in India, and the East India Company the means of conception. Many Company staff lived in the city, and in 1792 they formed their own club – the oldest outside Britain. Its main purpose was to arrange games between employees, and the first genuine match in India took place in 1804, Calcutta losing heavily to eleven Etonians of the Company. Robert Vansittart contributed 102 of the Etonians' 232, the first century on Indian soil. By 1825, the Calcutta club had occupied a plot of land on the eastern bank of the Hooghly River, between Government House and Fort William.

A decade later, the Earl of Auckland, George Eden, was appointed Governor General of India, and moved into Government House, along with his sisters, Emily and Fanny. The sisters were enchanted by the sight of the Calcutta club playing a team of naval officers on the maidan, and devoted the next six years to laying out enclosed, ornamental gardens between the river and the cricket ground. On the boundary furthest from the river stood a graceful, shady banyan tree, where passers-by could pause and watch the game. The locals felt it was a little piece of England.

By the middle of the nineteenth century, there were clubs at Madras, Bombay, Bhagalpur, and a second Calcutta club, at Ballygunge. Organised matches, though, were exclusive to the East India Company and the British armed forces. That changed in January 1862, when Bhagalpur made the 230-mile journey south to take on Calcutta: a prototype for inter-club cricket in the

James Brightman was charged with damaging a door, the property of Mr. Thomas North. The complainant said: "I went into my field, and saw the defendant and several others playing at cricket with the pieces of a door that had been broken." The defendant was ordered to pay the damage of 1s, a fine of 1s, and costs of 8s 6d. — *Rugby Advertiser*, 5 March subcontinent. Calcutta won the game handsomely – and their members became convinced that proper domestic cricket had a future in India.

After lengthy negotiations, Calcutta and Ballygunge merged at the start of 1864, and a Madras team were invited for a three-day game; the *Madras Times* requested subscriptions for their travelling expenses. The contest is now regarded by many Indians – though not by cricket's statistical authorities – as the first first-class match in the country.

At Calcutta, January 6, 7, 8. **Madras won by 61 runs. Madras 124** (H. L. Linton 67; R. S. Hills 5 wickets, G. Hills 4 wickets) **and 141** (P. P. Hutchins 32; G. Hills 4 wickets, R. S. Hills 5 wickets); **Calcutta 100** (R. Grant 43; F. Brandt 6 wickets, H. L. Linton 3 wickets) **and 104** (G. Hills 37; F. Brandt 5 wickets, H. L. Linton 5 wickets). *Toss not known.*

A letter was sent to George Parr, in Australia, requesting that the England team play Calcutta on their way home, but no reply was received. Perhaps that was for the best. "The Calcutta men have been disgracefully beaten on their own ground," thundered *Homeward Mail from India*. "We hope that before they invite any other eleven they will practise a little, and not field like so many clodhoppers." *Bell's Life* acidly remarked that "a superfluity of hospitality was not shown to the Madras eleven, who had the spirit to travel two thousand miles in quest of the game". Though the contest was a let-down, it was still considered newsworthy in England, where the *Illustrated London News* printed a portrait of the successful Madras team.

At the end of January, Bhagalpur visited again, and Calcutta obtained their first victory, by six wickets. They then took on a Civil Service XI, and had the worse of a draw, with J. D. McLean scoring 100 for the opposition.

But no sooner had club cricket gained a foothold in Calcutta, than it faced an existential threat. The officers at Fort William had long been jealous of the club's occupation of the land. In the 1840s, Major Abercrombie, the garrison's chief engineer, decided the cricketers had got above their station, and should be reminded that their ground existed more as a matter of favour than of right. The chief magistrate, W. H. Elliott, agreed: "I should be rejoiced to see the cricket enclosure removed."

Abercrombie and Elliott devised a ruse to force the issue: the construction of a new and entirely unnecessary road connecting Government House with the Calcutta Gate of Fort William – plumb through Eden Gardens and the cricket ground. There was already a road from Government House to Fort William, so the Governor General, James Broun-Ramsay, sided with the club.

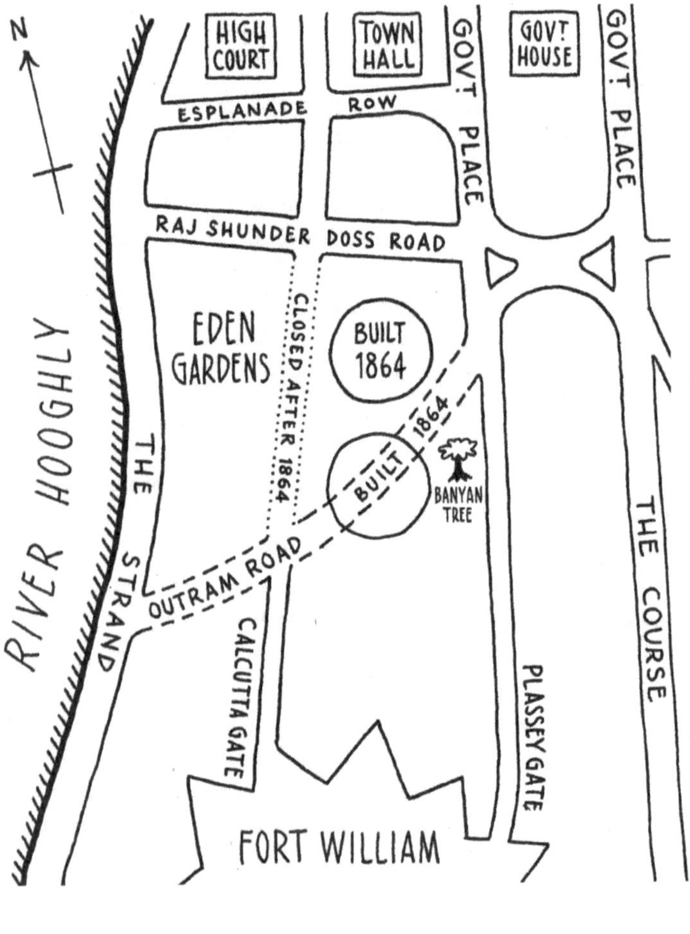

But in February 1864, once Broun-Ramsay was dead (as were George Eden and his sisters), it was announced that the work would go ahead. Before the cricketers had time to react, their ground was dug up. They appealed to Sir Cecil Beadon, Lieutenant Governor of Bengal, who issued his final verdict on 1 March.

"The tree is all sentiment," wrote Sir Cecil. "It is on the wrong side of the ground [from the gardens], and people have the afternoon sun in their eyes when they look at the game. I do not think that the inconvenience of the cricketers ought to induce an inferior arrangement of a road that will last for ever."

The cricket ground was relocated a hundred metres to the north, and linked to the Gardens. Ironically, this necessitated the destruction of the road between the Town Hall and Fort William, making the garrison *less* accessible. The members of the Calcutta Cricket Club found that the new location was vastly superior, even if one could no longer watch from beneath the banyan tree.

The troublesome road – Outram Road, now called Gostho Paul Sarani – survives today, and so do the Gardens, and the cricket ground. A ramshackle pavilion, just north of the banyan tree, was replaced by a grander edifice in 1871. Its teak-panelled Long Room was modelled on the Lord's pavilion. This building lasted longer than a century, but made way for the B. C. Roy Clubhouse as the ground expanded towards a capacity of 100,000 which made it, by the 1980s, the largest cricket stadium in the world. The original tree is no more, but its successors still provide shade at the westbound Eden Gardens bus stop, behind the Clubhouse.

> Football, for the healthy and strong, is an excellent exercise, but for the young or weak it is altogether dangerous. The exertion, the effort, the strain, is where they are least able to sustain it: in the abdomen, groin and loins. And if the boy be fairly endowed with pluck, his weakness will never be taken into reckoning when the ball is in view. Cricket is an exercise of a very different nature. Strength and daring are not among its requisites. It would be difficult to devise a game better fitted for recreation; the man who invented cricket deserves a statue to his memory. For the grand old warrior confessed, as he watched the Eton boys batting in their field – the field that led to his – "It was here that Waterloo was won." — *Orkney Herald*, 15 March

Parr may not have responded favourably to his invitation to Calcutta – assuming he received it at all – but when his Twelve arrived back in Melbourne on 1 March, a letter was waiting for him at Marshall's Hotel. It was from a Sydney businessman, offering the team £2,500 to play three matches at Sydney. The New South Wales administrators had caved in.

First, the team had a game at Castlemaine, so they took a northbound train the following morning. They started batting that afternoon, and it was lucky they took first innings, because the match barely made it to the third day.

At Castlemaine, March 2, 3, 4. **England won by an innings and 37 runs. ‡England 137** (J. W. Amos 3-32, C. Makinson 3-22); **Castlemaine XXII 54** (J. Jackson 4-11, T. Hayward 7-10, R. C. Tinley 9-28) **and 46** (R. C. Tinley 12-28, T. Hayward 8-13). *Anderson, recovering from seasickness, sat out. Wills umpired.*

It might have been better if Wills had played. As it was, only two of the local batsmen made it to double figures. This was a pity, since Castlemaine had made a name for themselves by beating beaten H. H. Stephenson's England team two years earlier, and much work had since been done to improve the playing area. All their stars of the 1861-62 game were playing; the result only proved how much better Parr's side was than Stephenson's. Castlemaine's humiliation was completed on the third afternoon when, owing to the early finish, their best XI took on Grace and Jackson. Grace scored 13 and Jackson nought, but Castlemaine were bowled out for two.

With a week to kill before the voyage to Sydney, Parr and Marshall organised an exhibition match at Melbourne. Parr took six England men and Marshall; Anderson captained another six, plus Wills. The remaining places were supposed to have been taken by local professionals, but they tried to increase their fee at the last minute, were rebuffed, and refused to participate. Into their shoes stepped eight inexperienced amateurs, but since this was an eleven-a-side fixture, it was later given first-class status (the earlier Parr v Anderson match, in Christchurch, was not given this honour, though it surely had better players).

Parr found himself with three Australians, plus an Irishman, Thomas Kelly, who would go on to become England's 12th international player, when he made his debut in the Second Test of 1876-77. Anderson's recruits also included an Irishman, Mathew Evanson O'Brien. He made nought and six, but then, he wasn't really a cricketer: after a stint as a police inspector, he returned to Dublin, qualified as a lawyer, then joined the gold rush in the Klondike.

At Melbourne, March 5, 7, 8. **Anderson's XI won by four wickets. ‡Parr's XI 153** (W. Caffyn 36; E. M. Grace 5-33, T. Hayward 3-38) **and 129** (W. Caffyn 40; T. W. Wills 4-34, E. M. Grace 4-36); **Anderson's XI 168** (T. Lockyer 44, A. Clarke 40; R. C. Tinley 7-76) **and 115-6** (G. Anderson 38, T. Lockyer 40*; G. F. Tarrant 4-63).

There was still time to relax, attend the theatre, and pose for team photographs and portraits ("they were all good likenesses except Hayward's", wrote Caffyn). Then came the three-day sail to Sydney, where the Twelve found their land-legs with a stroll along the coast – though seeing the wreck of the *Dunbar*, which had foundered five years earlier with the loss of 121 lives, can't have done Parr's anxiety much good.

The sickly Anderson struggled, too, with the heat and crowds, both of which were oppressive. "Each of us had a bodyguard of a thousand," he wrote. The New South Wales games were played at the Outer Domain – far more central than today's Sydney Cricket Ground – where a huge enclosure, and 3,000-seater stand, had been constructed. The total cost of staging the three games was estimated at £6,000, and since the land was public property, the city did not allow admission to be charged. Even so, the organisers expected to get their money back, and then some.

At Sydney, March 16, 17, 18, 19, 24. **England won by four wickets. New South Wales XXII 137** (R. C. Tinley 4-47, G. F. Tarrant 4-20, J. Jackson 5-15, W. Caffyn 3-13) **and 50** (G. F. Tarrant 8-27, J. Jackson 9-20); **‡England 128** (N. F. D. Thomson 4-26, G. Moore 4-66) **and 60-6**. *Anderson, being seasick, stood as umpire.*

A huge crowd – perhaps as many as 20,000 – watched the opening day, and were not disappointed by their team. Nat Thomson (who later opened the batting alongside Charles Bannerman in the first two Test matches) made 26, and former Surrey and Middlesex all-rounder Charles Lawrence hit 25.

New South Wales batted into the second day, reaching 137, as England stuck with slow bowling. When the tourists' turn came, they fell short, though Grace was unwell, and Parr was gripped by a second attack of erysipelas. A heavy shower made the pitch sticky, and New South Wales struggled to add to their lead of nine. By the fourth day, they were 37 for 16 – and then the rain returned with a vengeance. It hammered down for four days, but since the English were in town until April, there was no reason to call it a draw. The game finally resumed on Maundy Thursday – the ninth day on which play was scheduled – and England muddled their way to victory.

Two days later, the teams stepped on to the damp ground again. This time, they agreed on a three-day game – and if it couldn't be finished, so be it.

At Sydney, March 26, 28, 29. **Drawn. ‡New South Wales 102** (J. Jackson 4-22, G. F. Tarrant 5-35, R. C. Tinley 4-25, W. Caffyn 5-11, T. Hayward 3-2) **and 1-1; England 114** (O. H. Lewis 4-31, G. H. B. Gilbert 5-58). *Clarke umpired.*

It couldn't be finished. The teams tried everything, playing through the rain until they were ankle-deep in mud. England were again evenly matched, in terms of runs, if not numbers. Lawrence made another 25, then the New South Wales captain, George Gilbert – Grace's cousin – sent back five English batsmen. The tourists only took a first-innings lead when Parr, now very ill, staggered out at No. 10 and helped Tarrant add 18 for the last wicket. There was little action after that, but the Sydney public felt their team had done enough to show they might yet beat the English before the tour was over.

On Tuesday night, an outrage of almost unexampled atrocity was perpetrated at the village of Fiskerton, in Nottinghamshire. Richard Thomas had visited the site of the Sheffield flood on Monday, but instead of returning home, spent Tuesday drinking at the cricket-field in Newark. When he reached home, his father found fault with him for not returning according to promise. High words ensued, the son threatened his father with blows, and a chase took place around the house. Richard took a loaded double-barrel gun from the shelf, and killed both his parents. After being arrested, he said he should die on the scaffold like a dog. — *Bell's Life*, 31 March. *Thomas pleaded not guilty, but was convicted on 21 May, and executed at Nottingham on 10 August.*

Back in England, the new season was about to begin. There was almost no other sport to occupy a man's time – football was in its infancy – so matches began much earlier in the spring than they do today. *Bell's Life* reported that Good Friday, 25 March, was for many clubs the start of the season, but the earliest game (excepting those played on ice in January) was on 12 March, at Stubbington House in Hampshire, where schoolboys from Eton, Marlborough and Winchester split themselves into teams of Sloggers (34 and 20) and Anti Sloggers (57). *Bell's Life* had a correspondent there: "Those who 'failed to obtain' – and their name is legion – wish to plead want of practice and the deadness of the ground as an excuse."

Scoring was rarely easy in those days. The Laws of Cricket did not yet allow for boundaries, so the batters had to run until the ball was returned. Though one-day games rarely started before noon, the innings were so short that teams usually had time to bat twice. Fifties were scored about as often as hundreds are today; indeed, at club and village level, it was rare for a whole team to score 100, let alone an individual. The pitches were almost universally dreadful. An early-season game in Nottingham, featuring several first-class players, did not last very long. "Imagine the disappointment felt when, on play commencing, it was at once discovered that the pitch was useless for cricket," wrote the *Nottinghamshire Guardian*. "It is true that the whole ground had been mown, and the pitch rolled out, but the sun had done its duty, and the ground was as hard as nails. It would have required a roller of something like the weight of Juggernaut's car to have made an impression upon it. The result was that several players were struck on the head or other portions of their frame, and were frightened from any attempt to develop good cricket."

Good Friday in 1864 was cold, but that was no obstacle to recreation. It was one of only two Bank Holidays in the UK – the other being Christmas Day – and there was nothing to stay indoors for. In London, the *Morning Star* reported that "Clapham Common, Battersea Park, Blackheath, Peckham Rye, Primrose Hill and Victoria Park were numerously attended by lovers of the game". At Calthorpe Park in Birmingham, a game between Pickwick and Grange had to be abandoned because there were too many spectators.

Local newspapers were desperate to provide the fullest coverage they could obtain, even in the absence of proper matches. In Yorkshire, the *Tadcaster Post* published a report and full scorecard for a match between four labourers and four servants of Terrying Farm.

LABOURERS

1st innings		2nd innings	
J. Richardson b E. Metcalf	0	b E. Metcalf	0
G. Thompson c Blakeborough	1	c E. Metcalf	0
J. Robinson b E. Metcalf	1	b M. Metcalf	6
H. Cundall b E. Metcalf	3	b E. Metcalf	0
Total	**5**	Total	**6**

SERVANTS

1st innings		2nd innings	
J. Hare b Robinson	0	b Cundall	0
T. Blakeborough st Robinson	0	b Robinson	0
M. Metcalf b Robinson	0	b Robinson	0
E. Metcalf b Robinson	1	b Robinson	4
Total	**1**	Total	**4**

APRIL

As the English spring warmed up, the growing demand for cricketing news – especially during the long wait between despatches from Australia – pushed editors to publish anything they could get their hands on. Clubs' meetings and fixture lists were covered in the fullest detail. *Sporting Life* even sent a reporter to an Oxford University practice session.

> The turf was heavy, but so eager were all to be at it again, that each college ground was thronged by undergraduates. The balls whizzed about in all directions, and it was positively quite refreshing to again hear the good old cricket exclamations of "Look out there", "Mind your head, sir", "I really beg your pardon" and (rubbing his head) "All right, old fellow," and so on.

Not everything went so smoothly. A Nottingham side were planning to play a game in Paris later in the season, so arranged a practice session at the Forest New Ground. According to the *Nottingham Journal*, the plan did not meet with universal approval.

> Before long the policeman in charge of the ground appeared, and said he could not allow play to be continued, as it was not a match. But the cricketers had, it appears, previously paid the fee demanded for use of the ground, and were by no means disposed to finish their game in this abrupt manner. The policeman, therefore, stationed himself in front of the wicket, and some expressed a determination, unless he went away, to bowl at him. They dared him to pull up the wicket, and said if he did they should summon him before the magistrates. Considerable altercation took place, and when the players demanded that they should either be allowed to continue or that their money should be returned to them, the policeman stated that he had not got it, but had handed it over to some other officials. Ultimately the matter was arranged by the players making up a match with some of the bystanders, whereupon the policeman withdrew.

This was amusing news – but what the public really wanted were genuine games. The *Dundee Advertiser* gave them one: "The first match of the season came off in the Market Muir at Forfar, on Saturday afternoon, between the

Academy United and Thistle Clubs. The Thistle went first to the bat, but were put out with a score of 18. The Academy United then went in, and scored 64. At their second innings, the Thistle only succeeded in raising the former score to 48, thus leaving the Academy United victor by 16 runs and an innings." But the *Advertiser* quickly found out that you can't please everyone.

> Dear sir — I happened to be a spectator of the match (if such it can be called), and I write for the benefit of clubs in nearby towns who may think it worth their while to play a friendly match with their Forfar brethren, and to save them needless correspondence with the heroes of Saturday last who have taken to themselves the honour of leading the season. The match was played by boys about eight years old, with a fourpenny India-rubber ball, with neither umpire nor a full complement on either side, and with all the knowledge of (and attention to) the Laws of Cricket which characterise boys of their age.

The editor replied that he had assumed the match was from a club of standing because the boy who sent in the report had excellent handwriting.

Many players started with an internal match, such as between the first and second teams, or between the married and the single. East Yorks Rifle Volunteers attempted the latter kind, but the single men won easily, since only eight husbands could obtain permission to play. Other players took advantage of weak opponents. The Surrey professionals Thomas Humphrey and William Mortlock warmed up with a single-innings game against schoolboys in Kent: Mortlock carried his bat, and Humphrey took all ten wickets.

Some pushed the boat out for their opening day. The *Ashton Reporter* said of Hurst CC: "The field was decorated with flags, the Park Bridge Band came on the ground, and after the game the members were regaled with a large pie each, which was very much relished."

A daring few put their lack of preparation from their minds and organised a proper game, against proper opposition. Thornsett, in Derbyshire, probably

> Cricket in France is on the increase. Paris, Lyon, Le Havre, Boulogne and Calais each have a club, and number a few monsieurs who pick up the thing readily, and don't mind a hot ball. — *Freeman's Journal*, 5 April

regretted that decision, conceding 93 against Little Hayfield and being bowled out for six. Two works teams in Bristol – Derham Brothers and Bristol Schoolmasters' Club – must have blushed when extras top-scored in all four innings.

In some cases, there were matches without cricketers. Dozens of spectators turned out at Godalming when a poster advertised a single-wicket contest, only to return home when no players appeared. Kendal Mechanics' Institute had to take down bills stating that the tercentenary of the birth of Shakespeare would be marked by a special game at the club. In both cases, the advertisements were assumed to be the work of pranksters.

~~

At last, there came news of the England's last matches in Australia. In prospect, these were the biggest of the tour, and in practice, they did not disappoint.

New South Wales had played three games against Stephenson's touring team of 1861-62, joining forces with Victoria in two of them. In their sole outing as a genuine New South Wales side, captained by Gilbert, they had been soundly beaten. But this time, led by Lawrence, they held their own. There were runs for Lawrence, wickets for Gilbert, and both for Thomson.

At Sydney, April 2, 4, 5, 6. **England won by one wicket. ‡New South Wales XXII 68** (J. Jackson 7-21, T. Hayward 4-27, G. F. Tarrant 7-0) **and 83** (R. C. Tinley 10-33, T. Hayward 8-20); **England 75** (C. Lawrence 4-42, O. H. Lewis 5-14) **and 77-9** (C. Lawrence 6-48). *Clarke umpired.*

New South Wales chose to bat first, and spent the entire day – nearly 112 four-ball overs – accumulating 68. Thomas Lewis, born in Middlesex, scored 12, and his Sydney-born brother Oswald made 13. No one else managed more than six, and the last seven wickets added just three runs; Tarrant's entire spell was 35 balls, seven wickets, no runs. Next day, the English had painstakingly reached 39 for one when Oswald Lewis dismissed Grace, whose 20 ended up being the highest score of the game. Lewis and Lawrence kept England to a lead of just seven, but New South Wales were 15 for nine – seven of them ducks – when stumps were drawn. The local umpire was then called home: his two-year-old son had drowned in a water tub in the family's backyard.

On a downbeat third morning, the home batsmen grimly accumulated, until another collapse against Hayward, who took eight of the last ten wickets and finished with match figures of 15 for 20. England's target was 76, and the new-ball pairing of Oswald Lewis and Lawrence had them 18 for two at the close. The scores were level when the ninth wicket fell, in the 116th over, bringing Tinley to the wicket. At this point, he had 242 wickets on the tour, but only 35 runs. To him fell the honour of making the winning hit.

The following evening, Parr and his men bade farewell to New South Wales, and boarded a steamer, the *Wonga Wonga*, as night fell. They were only a few miles from shore when they hit a small sailing boat, the *Viceroy*. According to Caffyn, the English were having supper at the moment of collision – seasickness having not had time to kick in – and raced to the deck in a panic, with the exception of Parr ("utterly dazed and paralysed with alarm"), Jackson ("had done himself extra well at the farewell luncheon, and was fast asleep, not having the least idea that anything had happened") and Caesar ("behaved in a manner worthy of his name"). As a lifeboat was lowered to rescue the crew of the *Viceroy*, a terrified Tarrant jumped into it. The voyage of the *Wonga Wonga* was delayed by a day, and the rest of it was spent soothing nervous ladies – plus Parr and Tarrant – and trying to ward off mosquitoes. The only way to be sure of avoiding a bite was to sleep on deck, which gave several players a bad cold.

Marshall and his waiters spent 11 April administering pick-me-ups, before it was time for the party to take train ride round the bay to Geelong. On arrival, the ever-unfortunate Anderson found his luggage had not accompanied them.

At Geelong, April 12, 13. **Drawn. Geelong XXII 103** (R. C. Tinley 9-39, J. Jackson 3-18, G. F. Tarrant 5-25) **and 64-9** (G. F. Tarrant 3 wickets, J. Jackson 3 wickets); **England 135** (G. F. Tarrant 41, T. Hayward 35; T. W. Wills 6-49). *Toss not known. Anderson went back to Melbourne in search of his bags, then fell ill again.*

It was at Geelong, in 1859, that Thomas Austin had imported 24 rabbits from England. Within two decades, there were two billion, and Australian pasture was close to annihilation. Even by 1864, there were tens of thousands, although there was no time for Parr's Twelve to go hunting.

The match ought to have begun the previous day, but the delay incurred by the sea accident cut the playing time to two days. England did their best to push for victory, but the local team batted all the first day. They were strengthened by Marshall, Bryant and Wills, but it was one of Wills's associates who worked hardest. John Conway came in at No. 15, with the score 62 for 13, and 41 precious runs were added – of which Conway scored 31 (in 1876-77, he acted as the agent for James Lillywhite's England team in Australia, and dreamed up the fixture that would become the first Test match). Replying to Geelong's 103, England reached 92 for two, then collapsed against Wills. The match meandered to a draw, and the Twelve returned to Melbourne.

They were up bright and early – all except Anderson, once more confined to his bed – for a long trip to Maryborough, the reverse of the journey they had undertaken three months previously. The fixture was a third instalment of Anderson's XI v Parr's XI, without Anderson.

At Maryborough, April 14, 15, 16. **Anderson's XI won by 56 runs. ‡Anderson's XI 164** (E. M. Grace 37, G. F. Tarrant 35; T. Hayward 4-74, W. Caffyn 3-31) **and 74** (J. Jackson 3-23, T. Hayward 5-34); **Parr's XI 112** (J. Jackson 45, T. Hayward 32; J. Caesar 3-18, R. C. Tinley 6-59) **and 70** (R. C. Tinley 3-39, J. Caesar 6-31). *Anderson remained in Melbourne.*

Marshall took Anderson's place, and Tarrant assumed the captaincy; both teams borrowed five local players, mostly from the Maryborough side who had been thrashed in January. Tarrant had a half-decent one, John Freestone, whose first-innings 16 helped the team reach 164. Parr's team found Tinley as hard

On Sunday, four youths (William Crowther, John Millar, Alfred Chapple and Alfred Smith) were summoned before the Wells magistrates for damaging grass by playing cricket. The magistrates reprimanded the Sabbath breakers, and ordered them to pay the costs. — *Western Advertiser*, 6 April to face as the Australians had, and fell to a substantial defeat, losing the three-match series (of sorts) by two to one.

The third day ended early, so Grace invited Maryborough to select their best six, to take him on single-handed. It was agreed that he would bat first – and at the end of the day, he was still batting, 106 not out, the first century of the tour. The second came three days later.

At Ballarat, April 18, 19, 20. **Drawn. ‡England 310** (R. P. Carpenter 121, G. Parr 65; W. H. Greaves 3-24); **Ballarat XXII 128** (R. C. Tinley 8-72, T. Hayward 5-25, J. Jackson 6-15) **and 48-15** (R. C. Tinley 10-28). *Anderson was still in Melbourne.*

After another rough road journey, past Avoca and Eversley, the party arrived in Ballarat, where they would play the first of the two return fixtures that concluded their trip. Though Ballarat had Bryant, Greaves, Marshall and Wills, England reached 280 for five, with Carpenter making 121 and adding 157 for the sixth wicket with Parr. Tinley gave the home team no chance of winning, but they batted 105 overs in their first innings, and the game was drawn.

The final game was a re-run of the first, against Victoria at Melbourne. After the contretemps in March, there was uncertainty as to whether the local professionals would participate without a fee, but Bryant had eased tensions by playing at Geelong and Ballarat, and a letter from Greaves to the *Melbourne Herald* said they had all now agreed to play, if selected, for the honour of the colony. They were selected, of course.

At Melbourne, April 21, 22, 23. **Drawn. Victoria XXII 150** (J. Jackson 10-34, G. F. Tarrant 5-39) **and 83-17** (G. F. Tarrant 12-29, R. C. Tinley 3-23); **‡England 131** (W. Stewart 3-31, T. W. Wills 3-24). *Caesar umpired.*

There was just time to squeeze the game in before the Englishmen boarded the mail steamer on 25 April. They requested a day's rest after the game, so three days were allocated for play. Parr won the toss and put the Victorians in, but frequent showers meant they could only reach 117 for 17 on the first day. A late rally from Wills brought the score to 150, Jackson taking ten wickets. The English showed no haste, crawling to 131 in 168 overs, the only stand of note coming from Carpenter (27) and Parr (25). They were all out on the third afternoon and, though Tarrant clean bowled ten of the locals, it was clear the game would not be completed. At stumps, Victoria were 102 ahead with four wickets in hand. They begged for the game to continue, but to no avail: Parr insisted that his men have their day off. They boarded RMS *Bombay* late at night, and embarked early on 26 April. On top of their £50 tour advances, they pocketed at least £200 each.

Two of the touring party were not aboard. Grace had travelled up-country to stay with friends, a visit which *Sporting Life* claimed was "not unlikely to end in a matrimonial engagement". It didn't, though Grace was to marry four times back home. Caffyn had signed a £300-a-year contract to coach Melbourne Cricket Club. The rest, though, made it home in time to play in the bulk of the cricket season in England – where they found a rapidly changing cricketing landscape.

Up until 1864, county cricket had risen and fallen several times. The first inter-county match with first-class status took place between Surrey and Kent at Laleham Burway in 1773, the second year of first-class cricket. Hampshire also played that season, and the three teams faced each other on and off (with very occasional appearances by Essex and Middlesex) until the late 1790s.

Then came a drought of 28 seasons, from 1797 to 1824, with no first-class county cricket at all. The highest standard of the sport in those years was invitation games involving MCC and specially selected 'England' or 'Surrey' sides; the Gentlemen v Players fixture, pitting wealthy amateurs against hard-working professionals, began in 1806. Cricket's hinterland, though, was still those five southern counties. It rarely extended further north than London.

The catalyst for the first renaissance of county cricket, from 1825, was the new Sussex team (powered initially by the efforts of the Brighton Cricket Club, then led by William Lillywhite), who were involved in three-quarters of all matches over the next quarter of a century. The county game edged its way northward – Norfolk, Nottinghamshire, Yorkshire and Lancashire began to make appearances – so that by the mid-point of the century, ten counties had played first-class cricket.

In 1851, there were a record nine fixtures, the most since 1776. But then there was another decline – and a rapid one. The growing fame of Clarke's All England side, and the introduction of Wisden's breakaway United England team in 1852, captivated the public. Within four years, county cricket had shrunk to a tiny nucleus, with Kent, Surrey and Sussex the only fully functioning clubs. That summer's first-class programme had 24 matches: only two, at Newark and Salford, were staged north of Lord's, and just five were county games.

But another dawn was breaking, in the guise of the rapidly-spreading British railway network. Fast, efficient, affordable town-to-town travel meant that the best local players no longer had to wait for Clarke or Wisden's teams to come to them. They could now form their own representative sides, and travel to meet others.

And form them they did. County cricket burst into life again. Between 1856 and 1863, at least 18 counties fielded some sort of team. Kent, Surrey and Sussex were joined by Yorkshire and Hampshire as properly-constituted clubs. In 1864, seven more were voted into existence.

The English team were little more than three weeks into their sea voyage when the officials of Wellesbourne Cricket Club – from a village just east of Stratford-upon-Avon – met in Warwick and voted to change their name to Warwickshire. In January 1864, the Earl of Warwick was installed as president, 200 members paid the £1 subscription, and the *Birmingham Daily Gazette* reported that "the ground at Warwick will be enlarged to about twelve acres".

A week ago our townsmen were astonished by a placard announcing the sale of the cricket ground. The day before the sale, passers-by were still more astonished at seeing men at work, pulling down the pavilion and carrying the woodwork into an adjoining field. At the time of the sale, there was a large assemblage of people, expecting some explanation. When the auctioneer arrived, the members of the cricket club presented him with a receipt for £10, claiming they had already bought the pavilion, and were taking it with them to a new location. He declined to have anything more to do with what he called a "dirty transaction". — *Grantham Journal*, 16 April

Other clubs in the area were outraged that an ordinary village side chould decide, by simple resolution, to bestow on themselves the title of county club. No doubt they were delighted when, in March, the new club's ground arrangements fell through, and the *Gazette* published a plea for a place to play. And they were probably disappointed when, the following month, the Wellesbourne men got hold of a field on Hampton Road, just outside Warwick, opposite the racecourse. Soon, there was a pavilion, bar, and a veranda for a band. The ground became the modern home of Warwick CC.

The Lancashire team that previously played first-class games against Yorkshire was really Manchester Cricket Club under an assumed name. The county club proper was formed at the Queen's Hotel on 12 January 1864, but although there was a cricket ground at Old Trafford, it did not immediately become Lancashire's home. According to the *Manchester Courier*. "It was not intended at present to provide a playing ground, as there were many good ones in the county, the use of which could be readily obtained. The matches would be held at Manchester, Liverpool, Preston, Blackburn and other places."

An annual subscription of one guinea (£1 1s) was considered trifling, and there were soon more than 100 members. Lancashire's first match was against Birkenhead Park CC at Warrington, and though there was no first-class opposition until the following year, there were several good contests against gentlemen's sides. "It is the purpose of the club to obtain for Lancashire such a position in cricket as Kent and Sussex at present hold," wrote the *Liverpool Mercury*. "This will be a work of time, but there is no reason why it should not be accomplished." In little more than a decade, Lancashire were up there.

Various clubs in and around north London had played first-class games under the name of Middlesex as early as the eighteenth century. A formal club, though, did not appear until a meeting at the London Tavern in Bishopsgate, on 2 February 1864. The *Evening Standard* welcomed this development, somewhat exaggeratedly insisting that Middlesex was "the only cricketing county in England that has no club".

That first Middlesex meeting made two controversial decisions, at least as far as MCC were concerned. The first was that the county ground should not be

Lord's, but the Cattle Market in Islington, where a year's rent, including upkeep of the field, would cost £250 – a good deal cheaper than hiring Lord's. The second upset was an agreement with Sussex that, when they visited London in 1864, they would replace their MCC fixture with one against Middlesex. The Sussex secretary, Bridger Stent, said "he did not like to spend £80 when they got nothing for it", and his committee wholeheartedly agreed: "The Lord's pitch was so bad that the ball jumped from the pitch into the long stop's hand frequently. The men were very much knocked about, and did not care to go again. The ground was a disgrace to any Sussex common."

This was a colossal slight, though not without basis in reality. The Lord's pitch was among the worst in first-class cricket, and MCC evidently liked it that way. It did not have a mechanical mower until the 1850s, and even then, a posse of committee men crept out one evening and destroyed it. A heavy roller was not purchased until 1870. Sussex resumed their visits to Lord's in 1866, but Middlesex did not make a home there until 1877, and then only when the Cattle Market, then Prince's Ground in Chelsea, fell into the hands of the builders.

A casual cricket historian might be forgiven for concluding that the vogue for county club formation extended, in 1864, only as far as Warwickshire, Lancashire and Middlesex. They are big clubs today. But there were four more. Two days after the Bishopsgate meeting, a gathering at the Ivy Bush Hotel, Carmarthen, lamented the absence of a county club in Wales. Carmarthenshire was voted into being, *Bell's Life* reporting "60 to 70 members" and that "the political colours of the club have been blended to compose the ribbon".

The Carmarthen secretary, Charles Bishop, was not a progressive man. He told the meeting that tradesmen and the working classes were to be prevented from joining, because "when uneducated people are admitted, harmony and good feeling in county matches are sometimes forfeited". A writer to the *Carmarthen Journal* had misgivings: "I am sure Mr. Bishop will find considerable difficulty in bringing out a creditable team, composed entirely of gentlemen who are not in some way connected with trade. Indeed it is a well-known fact that the best cricketers in the county are so connected, while the best bowlers are actually of the working classes."

Later in February, a village team in Oxfordshire decided to follow the example of Wellesbourne CC and unilaterally anoint themselves as their county's representative team. Before 1864, the only reason anyone had heard of Deddington CC was because, several years earlier, a rabid dog had interrupted a game: a player stunned it with a bat, a farmer shot it, and the teams buried it on the boundary. Now these enterprising men restyled their modest club as Oxfordshire.

An epistolary argument erupted in *Sporting Life*. 'A Cowley Cricketer' backed Deddington, insisting they were "only club in the whole shire worthy of the name". When a reply from 'An Oxonian Cricketer' suggested this was nonsense, 'Cowley' pointed out that nine-tenths of the gentlemen cricketers of Oxfordshire played for Deddington, and suggested that 'Oxonian' try and find a team that could beat them: "Knowing how hopeless a task he has before him, I with these few remarks bid him goodbye, and leave him alone in his glory."

Bedfordshire, formed at the King's Arms Inn, Bedford, were up and running by the end of April, with practice every Tuesday and Friday at five o'clock. The first game pitted the best XI (100 and four for none) against the next XXII (55 and 56). But the club had problems settling on a ground: their first location, on Goldington Road, was quickly deemed unplayable; their second choice, at Bedford Grammar School, met with little enthusiasm from the school board. They were still forlornly advertising for help in September.

Dear sirs, I understand that the Ramsfort Cricket Club is extinct this year, and that it will not be standing forth in the noble game this season. It is a great pity that cricket should meet its doom so soon in County Wexford. Yours faithfully, 'Pollypus'. — Letter to the *Wexford Independent*, 16 April

My dear sir, I was greatly surprised to find that any individual would disgrace himself by the name 'Pollypus', meaning a four-footed animal, but it fully proves what an intellectual mind he has got. He ought to be ashamed of his ill-contrived and contaminated tissue of falsehoods. The Ramsfort Cricket Club will appear this season as well as last – and if we must contend with 'Pollypus', then let us meet on the cricket field, with bat and ball. Yours faithfully, J. Clarke. — Letter to the *Wexford Independent*, 20 April

Next came Suffolk, formed at the Angel Hotel, Bury St Edmunds, in midsummer – after Parr's men had returned home – though the club fielded only a gentlemen's eleven for its first couple of years. This may in part have been due to problems with the ground: the £15-a-year offer of a farmer's field on Northgate Street turned out to be too good to be true, so Suffolk accepted an offer to play at Fornham Park, the country estate of Sir William Gilstrap. It was perhaps not the sort of place you brought any old fellow.

The 1864 first-class programme comprised a record 46 games, and there was no longer a southern bias: fixtures were played at Bradford, Manchester, Middlesbrough, Nottingham, Sheffield and Sleaford. County cricket accounted for 24 games – more than half the season. There were eight first-class counties, referred to by more than one cricket historian as the "octarchy": the pre-1851 ten, plus Cambridgeshire, but minus Essex, Lancashire and Norfolk, who made do with club cricket.

Not all of the octarchy operated in the same way. Nottinghamshire and Yorkshire had a highly localised model, built around professionals, men of the county who earned a living playing for its club. Other clubs focused on amateurs, with a paid hack or two to do the bowling. Middlesex and Sussex tended this way, and to some degree Kent. Hampshire and Surrey were somewhere between the two. Cambridgeshire, a new team run by three of England's touring party (Carpenter, Hayward and Tarrant) was the outlier.

Though almost every local newspaper carried match scores, the most detailed reports were published by the *Sporting Gazette* and *Sporting Life*, plus the *Evening Standard* for games at Lord's or The Oval. *Bell's Life* also had substantial coverage, much of it from Fred Lillywhite.

> The first match of the Paris Cricket Club was played last week in the Bois de Boulogne. Mr. Sparks, the indefatigable secretary, is doing his best to introduce this game into fashion, and the club already shows a capital list of members. Cricket will, however, be of slow growth, we fear. In fact, we cannot imagine a denizen of the Boulevards standing up against a strong bowler. He would much rather go out with his friend, and risk *un mauvais quart-d'heure*, than be shot at in such a manner. — *Londonderry Sentinel*, 19 April

In April, sports reporting was revolutionised by an agreement between two telegraph companies – the Electric and International, and the Magnetic Telegraph – to transmit cricket scores over their networks. This only heightened the sense of anticipation, and not just when it came to first-class cricket.

All over England and Wales, second-class teams (as they were then called) took to the field in 1864. Huntingdonshire hosted Bedfordshire in a one-day game at the exquisitely named Turnip Piece ground. Buckinghamshire had home and away games with Middlesex, drawing at Newport Pagnell but losing at Islington. Cheshire played more than a dozen matches, though their only county games were two gentlemen's fixtures with Shropshire, whose only proper county opposition, in turn, were Montgomeryshire, who also played Ceredigion, triumphing by one run. Newly-founded Carmarthenshire played Breconshire at Dolgarreg, Pembrokeshire at Tenby, and Glamorganshire at The Gnoll in Neath, where county cricket is still played. Warwickshire – or rather, Wellesbourne – beat not only Staffordshire, but also Lancashire and Hampshire.

Some sides, like Denbighshire, Herefordshire and Hertfordshire, played only club cricket. Gloucestershire were at that time called West Gloucestershire, run by Teddy Grace and his family, while Oxfordshire (that is, Deddington) managed to get a side together only once, for the purpose of a spring fixture with the University. Northumberland, conversely, were very active and very strong. They didn't just host United England, they beat them, thanks to an extraordinary hundred by John Grey – arguably the innings of the season, at any level of the game.

Several counties played only as gentlemen's elevens: Devon's beat Cornwall's and Dorset's, and also thrashed MCC at Lord's. Lincolnshire's stuffed Yorkshire's, Suffolk's drew with Norfolk, and Warwickshire's beat Northamptonshire's twice. One way or another, 36 out of the 52 counties in England and Wales fielded representative teams in 1864. And by the end of the year, Yeovil were considering renaming themselves Somerset. County cricket had grown twelvefold in less than a decade.

MAY

Bowling styles had been causing controversy since the seventeenth century, and posterity credits two men with starting all the nuisance. The first was Hambledon's Tom Walker, who in the late 1700s became bored with the traditional method of rolling the ball along the ground as fast as possible, and started lobbing it up, trying to impart spin when it bounced. His team-mate, William Beldham, wrote: "When, in 1792, All England played Kent, I did feel so ashamed of such baby bowling," but conceded that Walker was a nightmare to face. Later, Walker added pace with a jerk from the elbow, which led to the introduction of the anti-throwing law, after an MCC ruling of 1816.

Bouncing the ball remained legal, which led to a more enduring debate: how high should the hand be allowed to rise? John Willes, from Kent, had learned cricket by playing against his sister, Christina, in the family's barn. Both bowled round-arm, though suggestions that Christina did so because she wore a hooped skirt seem fanciful. The style caught on, and cricket's underarm tradition – though not specifically enshrined in the laws – was eroded. The 1816 decree required the hand to be lower than the elbow at the point of delivery, but that was by no means the end of the matter.

In 1822, Willes was no-balled while playing for Kent against MCC. He threw the ball down, left the field, mounted his horse, and rode away from Lord's – and from cricket. But other bowlers of repute, such as William Lillywhite, continued to push the limit of the law. In 1829, MCC introduced Law X, stipulating that the hand could now be *level* with the elbow – but no higher. True round-arm bowling was now legal.

George Middleditch, a boy living in Mill Lane, was charged under the Juvenile Offenders Act with stealing a cricket ball, belonging to the Bury & West Suffolk Cricket Club. The ball in question was deposited, as usual, in a locker in the club's storage booth. C. Kemp, who has charge of the booth, made inquiries, and found that a lad named Welham saw the defendant break open the locker, but did not witness the abstraction of the ball. The prisoner attempted to lay the guilt on Welham. — *Bury and Norwich Post*, 10 May

Encouraged by the greater bounce that came with a higher release point, bowlers lifted their hands higher and higher. The debate raged, and MCC caved in again: in 1835, Law X raised the limit to shoulder height. But still the bowlers were not satisfied, and still the hand crept upwards.

On 26 August 1862, the second day of Surrey against an England XI at The Oval, Ned Willsher was no-balled six times in succession by John Lillywhite. There was some irony in Lillywhite being the son of a man who had done so much to advance the cause of round-arm bowling, but Willsher saw little to smile about. He stormed off the field, accompanied by eight team-mates. Lillywhite refused to change his mind, and play was abandoned for the day. The game only continued when a new umpire was appointed.

For *Sporting Life*, this was too much. A series of scathing editorials, in the run-up to the 1863 season, left no doubt as to where the blame lay.

> Everybody who takes the slightest interest in the game will recollect the commotion that was caused at The Oval last year, when an honest and conscientious umpire (John Lillywhite) took upon himself to vindicate Law X by no-balling one of the best cricketers living (Ned Willsher).
>
> Law X has been practically ignored for years. But MCC evidently feel themselves incompetent to grapple with the question. They hesitate to take any active steps towards removing that portion which refers to the height of the hand – or of enforcing the law as it now stands. They have thrown no end of responsibility upon the umpires, who in minor matches are notoriously incompetent.
>
> It is clear to us that the time has arrived when a Cricket Parliament, or congress, ought to be instituted, so that every shire which boasts a county club shall be represented. A meeting of this body should be held annually, to consider what (if any) alterations to the laws may have become necessary during the past season.

Stung by the criticism, MCC called their own meeting, at which the secretary presented seven letters from county clubs, supporting the alteration of Law X to allow delivery above shoulder height – in other words, to permit overarm bowling. There were three letters against. The passages from *Sporting Life* were even read out, yet there was little appetite for change. The secretary actually proposed a motion to make head height the limit, and an amendment was tabled to abolish the limit altogether. But both were voted down, and Law X was unchanged. The meeting then busied itself with an amendment to the lbw law, which was passed – only to be rescinded a couple of weeks later.

"The mountain had brought forth a mouse," wrote *Sporting Life*, whose reporter had attended the meeting. "It was admitted that a very large balance of opinion, gleaned from the leading clubs throughout the Kingdom, was in favour of an alteration to the law – but those opinions were disregarded. Why, then, were they ever sought?"

MCC gave instructions to all umpires officiating at Lord's that Law X was to be strictly enforced. "But they did nothing of the sort," wrote *Sporting Life*. "In the very first great match that followed, at which half the world had assembled to witness the way in which MCC would put their own pet law to a practical test, only one or two bowlers had got their arms down. The others were obviously unfair, but no no-balling took place, and the public went away sadly disappointed." Then, in July, the umpires suddenly went the other way: in front of thousands of spectators at Lord's, Cambridge's Tom Collins was no-balled five times in a row for delivering above shoulder height in the Varsity Match.

The coming of 1864 brought little respite for the beleaguered MCC committee. The *Sporting Life* campaign for decision-making to be taken out of

House of Commons, 12 May. Mr. Cox [Liberal, Finsbury] said a petition had been presented complaining that a portion of Battersea Park had been handed over to the Civil Service Cricket Club for their exclusive use. He was informed that the club consisted of 230 members, and that 19,000 square yards of ground had been set apart for them. Another portion, of 18,000 square yards, was allotted to another club with 600 or 700 members. A third portion, which was of no use whatever, was given to the general public for cricket. Mr. Carnegie [Liberal, Forfarshire] replied that the Civil Service had spent a great deal of money on their ground in Battersea Park, and had made it worth something, whereas the public space, being constantly knocked about, was in very bad condition. If the general public were to play on the Civil Service ground, it would soon be worth very little. — *Bell's Life*, 14 May their hands, and placed under the remit of a Cricket Parliament, had received support from clubs and newspapers in almost every cricketing county. Sussex secretary Bridger Stent, who (in spite of his criticism of the Lord's pitch) had previously called MCC's administration "tolerably satisfactory", suggested that the counties should now participate in decision-making at Lord's. MCC considered that idea risible, so Sussex threw in their lot with the revolutionaries. So did Surrey and Kent, plus the *Evening Standard* and *Daily Telegraph.*

The *Sporting Gazette*, though, called its rival publication's plan "a crude suggestion" which "contains the choicest materials for impotence and ultimate dissolution", while the *Illustrated Sporting News* began with "insane" and finished with "a waggon load of rubbishing bunkum". *The Era* was equally dismissive.

THE ERA'S PROPOSALS FOR CRICKET IN 1864

A few things that are wanted	**A few things that are not wanted**
More energy among the MCC committee	A Cricket Parliament
Early publication of fixture lists	Disputes between officials and professionals
Punctuality in commencing play	Time wasted at luncheon or between innings
The Winchester XI at Lord's again	Unfinished matches
Rugby, Cheltenham and Marlboro' Elevens at The Oval	Matches against odds at Lord's or The Oval
	Violated laws
An impartially written history of public schools' matches	Matches of 1,000 runs
	Single wicket matches
More county matches	Swiping
Accommodation for the press	Cigars and pipes when at play

Some members of MCC began a letter-writing campaign, spreading the rumour that talk of a Parliament had come to nothing. A writer to *Sporting Life* accused the Surrey secretary of "finding his vantage ground from which to assail the supremacy of the liege lords of cricket ... add a little jealousy, a little injudicious bottle-holding, and you have the whole component parts of the quarrel". Several letters to *Bell's Life* insisted the Parliament scheme was over.

This was wishful thinking. One county meeting after another passed unopposed resolutions in favour of a Parliament. Additional proposals included a central panel of neutral umpires, and minimum standards for pitches – a thinly-veiled attack on the playing surface at Lord's.

Up to this point, MCC had regarded *Bell's Life* as an ally. They submitted an 1864 fixture list for publication on 16 January, but sent nothing to *Sporting Life*. So they must have been stunned when, alongside the fixtures, *Bell's Life* launched its own broadside.

> MCC is the head of the cricket community. It has several hundred members, comprising the best of our amateur players, who pay an annual subscription of three guineas each, and its receipts from gate money are very great. Within the last two years, Lord's has become a fashionable lounge. Not only the cricketer, but the gentle and gay gather there. It is increasing in fashion. With such a position, and such means at its command, the MCC has duties to fulfil. They are sadly discharged.
>
> This great club plays upon a ground which not only prevents good cricket, but renders the game absolutely unsafe to limb and almost to life. During the whole of 1863, no good wicket was to be found at Lord's. Away from the centre of the ground, you would not know that you were on a cricket field. How can a fieldsman run in with a dash when he has to contend against ridge and furrow and rut?
>
> Turn from the ground to the pavilion. There, things are worse. So small is the building that no member, unless he is on the committee, is allowed to introduce a friend. Inconveniently built, out of repair, and with the smallest of retiring rooms, it is scarcely possible to find a more dreary-looking or worse adapted cricket pavilion than the one at Lord's. But bad as the pavilion is, far worse is the fare. At no country match can one find anything worse than the slovenly luncheons and slip-shod attendance that exist at Lord's. This evil is not to be excused on the ground of cheapness; nor is it ever mitigated by the civility of those who manage these arrangements. When a complaint is made to a committeeman, he will shrug his shoulders, and tell you of a higher power he cannot control.

Sir — The committee of the North Durham Cricket Club have refused to allow the Sunday School children to have their picnic in their field this year. This will cause the teachers a great deal of trouble, owing to the distance to the Gateshead Cricket Club, which has been granted for the occasion. The children will have to have eat indoors, and not in the field, the distance being too great to carry the tea. — Letter to the *Newcastle Daily Chronicle*, 17 May

As if things were not bad enough, it now transpired that there might, very soon, not even be a ground. Thomas Lord had sold the original lease to William Ward in 1825, and Ward had sold it to a Middlesex player, James Dark, in 1835. In 1860, the freehold was auctioned, but Dark could not persuade MCC to bid for it, and the land was bought by Isaac Moses, a property developer, for £7,000.

In March 1864, MCC's decision came back to bite them: Dark decided to sell up, and Moses decided to build. If MCC wanted to stay, they would have to pay – and the price tag would be substantially more than £7,000. By the spring, they were fighting a battle on two fronts: against the press, over their authority, and against Moses, for their ground.

At a huge meeting at Lord's on 16 April, the MCC committee informed their members that Dark had consented to sign his lease over to them, provided that they pay off the remaining term of the lease – £425 a year for the next 19 years – plus a lump sum of £11,000. Moses was then prepared to offer MCC a 99-year lease at £550 per year. Urgent improvements to the ground and pavilion brought the total immediately required past £20,000.

So began the mammoth task of raising what would, in today's money, be well over £2 million. The one crumb of comfort to the MCC committee was the rapidly approaching cricket season. May brought their annual matches at Cambridge and Oxford Universities, plus the All England v United England fixture, which guaranteed a capacity crowd. Life memberships went on sale for £30, debentures for £50, and when the Prince of Wales donated 100 guineas, the great and the good were falling over each other to support this worthy cause. As the first-class cricket season began, the required sum had been reduced to £12,500. By the end of the year, it was £5,000.

At Cambridge, May 12, 13. **Cambridge University won by six wickets. ‡MCC 108** (F. G. Pelham 5-43) **and 172** (J. Perkins 32*, H. E. Bull 46; T. S. Curteis 4-62); **Cambridge University 230** (C. G. Lyttelton 128, M. T. Martin 53; J. Grundy 6-90) **and 54-4**.

The opening game, at Fenner's, went badly for MCC. They had engaged three star professionals, but none played a winning hand: Tom Hearne almost immediately received a vicious blow, was bowled for nought, and could not field. After MCC capitulated for 108, James Grundy and George Wootton did almost all the bowling, but having reduced Cambridge to ten for three, they could not contain Charles Lyttelton. His century was one of two in his first-class career; he never played for a county, but appeared for several gentlemen's teams between 1861 and 1867. He became MP for East Worcestershire in 1868, was elevated to the Lords in 1876, and was MCC president from 1886 to 1887. Grundy worked his way through the rest of the order, restricting the students' lead to 122, but another failure by Hearne left MCC with little to defend on the second day. Cambridge needed 54 to win, and it says much for the skill of Grundy and Wootton that the chase occupied 45 overs.

The three professionals then travelled to London for the first big game of 1864: All England against United England, for the benefit of the Cricketers' Fund Friendly Society. To all intents and purposes this was the Lord's curtain-raiser for the season, though MCC had played a warm-up game against the Knickerbockers a week earlier. That was a rainy draw, though there had been sufficient play for the *Sporting Gazette* to admire the batting of a Canadian, Lieutenant Nesbit Willoughby Wallace: "He hit like a trooper and ran like a deer. He struck one from Grundy over the wall for six, and the ball knocked holes into the glass of a conservatory."

> Sir — Some time ago, your paper contained the report of a cricket match played at Teignmouth between the elevens of a club styling themselves Teignmouth United Cricket Club. The cricket club of Teignmouth is Teignmouth Cricket Club, and has been established for many years. It contains among its members many of the principal gentlemen of the town and neighbourhood. The club which styles itself the Teignmouth United Cricket Club has within the past month been formed, and consists of a few youths who have gathered together a bat and ball, and are daily on the Den playing at all hours, to the great annoyance of the residents near. Their language and conduct have been commented on at local meetings. The matches are made up between themselves, and to assist them in getting the elevens the aid of mere children, as young as eight, are called into requisition. Some of these children can scarcely hold the bat. When you again receive a report from the Teignmouth United Cricket Club, you should wisely commit it to the waste basket, or to the flames. — Letter to the *Western Daily Mercury*, 19 May

Since the teams' 1857 rapprochement, they had played 14 games, including a hastily arranged fixture on the North America tour: six wins by All England, six by United England, and two draws. Even though the very best players were still making their way back from Australia, the closeness of the teams meant feverish anticipation and a packed ground.

At Lord's, May 16, 17, 18. **United England won by two wickets. ‡All England 218** (G. Bennett 39, R. Daft 44, H. H. Stephenson 34, C. Brampton 45; R. Iddison 3-30) **and 166** (G. Wootton 60; T. Sewell 4-44, F. W. Bell 4-40); **United England 181** (T. Sewell 55, G. R. Atkinson 32*; E. Willsher 5-55) **and 206-8** (W. Mortlock 65, R. Iddison 44; G. Wootton 3-38).

The weather was splendid, and as many as 4,000 spectators watched All England compile 218 on the first day, Grundy going wicketless. Willsher, amid widespread speculation that he would be no-balled again, took five wickets as United England fell to 92 for eight, then met resistance in the form of Tom Sewell and George Atkinson, who lifted the total to 181. All England added just 166 to their lead of 37, and would have managed still less had Wootton – who had batted last in the first innings – not mustered 60 priceless runs. United England required 203, which seemed beyond them when they slid to 40 for three, Hearne being caught off Willsher for the second time in the game. But Mortlock stood firm. He hit one ball past square leg, through the gateway, out of the ground, across the road, and into a garden wall opposite; seven runs were scored for it. After Mortlock finally departed, Sewell saw United England's chase through. £220 was raised for the Cricketers' Fund. The very next morning, Hearne, Grundy and Wootton took the field for MCC at Oxford.

At Oxford (Magdalen), May 19, 20. **Drawn. ‡Oxford University 439** (T. Case 42, E. Tritton 110, F. W. Wright 32, E. Davenport 83, R. A. H. Mitchell 103, J. S. Frederick 39); **MCC 134** (H. E. Bull 43) **and 82-5.**

Oxford ran up a colossal total, keeping MCC in the field all day. Edward Tritton hit a hundred in his maiden first-class innings, earning himself a call-up for Middlesex's inaugural first-class match, in June. Richard Mitchell, the captain, also made a century. MCC were blown away for 134, and had to follow on 305 behind, but time ran out before Oxford could claim victory. The three professionals managed a total of 72 runs in the game.

For MCC, May had brought one disappointment after another. Criticisms of their decision-making and ground were now joined by concerns over their playing strength, and their plight looked all the more forlorn when viewed alongside the remarkable growth of another club, just ten miles away. Southgate CC were built around the seven Walker brothers, who allied cricketing skill with collective bargaining power. They had made Southgate the strongest club side of the 1860s, and had been instrumental in ensuring that the new Middlesex club – for which they all appeared – would be based at Islington rather than Lord's. When the Oxford students played their first away fixture of 1864, it was not to Lord's they travelled, but to Southgate, where they faced a team containing eight bona fide county cricketers. This was stronger opposition than MCC could muster, and the drawn match was subsequently accorded first-class status – as were seven other Southgate games during the decade.

Other teams, still shaking off the winter rust, fell some way short of that standard. Norwich Grammar School eased into the season with a match against Thorpe Lunatic Asylum. According to the *Norfolk News*: "The Asylum were ten patients and their doctor. The School made 41 and 7, the Asylum 116. Culling took nine wickets, Girling seven, and Dr. Hills was bowled for nought."

A match at Preston found several players still apparently hibernating: "The wickets were to be pitched at eleven o'clock, but in consequence of only two or three of the Manchester players putting in an appearance before that hour, it was necessary to delay until the arrival of the next train, thus throwing away two valuable hours. When the train arrived, shortly after one o'clock, it was found that only two or three more of the Manchester men were on it."

> Three youths, Woods, Palmer and Maslin, stole a cricket ball, value 3s, belonging to A. J. S. Wartley, an Eton schoolboy. Woods pleaded guilty to receiving the ball, and was given six weeks' imprisonment. Maslin was also sentenced to six weeks, and Palmer a week, as well as to be privately whipped six times with a birch rod. — *Windsor and Eton Express*, 21 May

In Ireland – at that time, part of the UK – the Viceregal Club played its opening fixture, though *Saunders's Newsletter* was more interested in the presence of the Lord Lieutenant of Ireland: "It gives us great pleasure to inform our readers that that the Earl of Carlisle is quite restored to health, and was able to sit outside for the entire match – as usual, keeping score." His Excellency may have seen out the game, but he did not last the year.

The greatest cricketing novelty of the spring was the Nottingham team's tour to France; several London newspapers sent correspondents to cover it.

> The Nottingham team are spending the Whitsuntide holidays in Paris, and astonishing the weak minds of the Paris Cricket Club, and the natives generally, by their batting and bowling. Yesterday, 16 May, they scored 175, in response to the 21 obtained by their Parisian opponents. We cannot say rivals. The Paris Club have been honoured by having the Emperor's name inscribed in its roll of members, with a subscription of 1,000 francs. — *Sporting Life*

> The Emperor passed by, and the players lined up to receive him, and cheered vociferously. The Emperor seemed much pleased, and waved his hat to them for a long time. But the match created not the slightest interest among the natives. A French soldier watching thought "it might be a nice game if you understood it". — *Field*

> Heavy bets were made that Paris, in their second innings, would not get more than 30, and singularly enough, 30 was the exact score. Paris took their beating with perfect good humour. The ground is a pretty lawn surrounded by a wood; every ball that goes into the brush (which is rather too near) counts for only two runs. Another ornament to the ground was a very fat umpire, whom I understand to be Mr. Hickling, the keeper of the Trent Bridge ground at Nottingham. — *Globe*

Paris then had two much closer contests with the Warwickshire Knickerbockers. They narrowly lost the first but, after a day of coaching from their visitors, won the second by ten wickets. Now the French took notice. The *Lettre de Paris* opined that "it is lawful to be instructed by a foe," while the *Moniteur* informed its readers that cricket balls were the same dimensions as "the cannon-ball projected by a 36-pounder", and claimed that the Knickerbockers were "a team of the eleven most famous players known".

JUNE

It was widely believed that 1864 would be a watershed season. *Sporting Life* called it "the most important that has yet occurred since cricket had its origin upon the Hampshire Downs nearly a century and a half ago". It added that the county game, which ten years earlier was being buried, was now "admitted on all hands to constitute the foundation tone of the entire fabric". The cricket press previewed all the teams.

> That **Cambridgeshire**, with her brace of brilliant batsmen [Carpenter and Hayward] and effective tearaway bowler [Tarrant], should play but two matches last season was a cause of regret to many. They could not play Surrey for want of funds. This season, we should like to find them in the thick of the fights.
>
> **Hampshire** are perhaps wise in confining their operations to the southern counties, the expense involved by journeys into northern latitudes being heavier than the club is presently justified in incurring.
>
> Although the motto 'Invicta' does not hold good as regards **Kent** in matters cricketical, the old county always comes out boldly, and quails not before any antagonist. But we regret to say that the team (whose professional cricketers are proverbial for their civility and uniform good conduct) will this year lose the services of their wicketkeeper, Harry Fryer, who met with an unfortunate accident some time since, by being thrown from a cart, which deprived him the sight of one of his eyes. [In the event, Fryer did play, but not as wicketkeeper.]
>
> **Middlesex**, the newest county, has come out strong, and has, like Hampshire – and we presume from similar prudential reasons – entered into engagements only with the home counties. We shall be much mistaken if Middlesex do not very soon rank amongst the leading counties of England.
>
> No district of England produces a more abundant crop of professional cricketers, or ranks higher in cricket circles, than **Nottinghamshire**. The revival of their match with Surrey is a circumstance which will be hailed with unfeigned satisfaction by all cricketers.
>
> The **Surrey** programme is, as usual, a formidable one. They contend with Sussex, Nottinghamshire, Hampshire, Kent and Yorkshire at The Oval. Cambridgeshire and Middlesex are the only cricket counties omitted from their list.

> **Sussex** have always issued an excellent bill of fare, and with such a splendid ground, equalled only in texture and smoothness by the bowling-greens of the north, it would be strange if some fine cricket was not there displayed. The committee have decided not to play MCC this season, because when Sussex played at Lord's in 1863 the ground was so bad that the men were very much knocked about. They did not care to go again. The secretary, Mr. Stent, reported a balance in hand of £6 13s 7d, which was the smallest he had known. He proposed not to play in the north, or the expenses would be heavier. A home game cost £30 to stage; home-and-away fixtures nearly £80.
>
> No programme has been announced by **Yorkshire** that we are aware of, but we may deduce that the team will play, since the Sheffield and Bradford committees have appeared as the promoters of contests with the celebrated elevens of Surrey and Nottinghamshire.

A week-long stay in London by the Sussex team produced the first two county matches of the summer. Notwithstanding the retirement of Wisden, they were at full strength, and had a good chance of winning at The Oval, since Surrey were still awaiting the return of Caesar and Lockyer from Australia.

SURREY v SUSSEX

At The Oval, June 2, 3, 4. **Drawn.** **‡Sussex 328** (C. H. Smith 95, G. Wells 82, John Lillywhite 49*, R. Fillery 40; T. Sewell 3-73, F. P. Miller 4-69) **and 101-2** (C. H. Smith 35*, John Lillywhite 64); **Surrey 291** (T. Humphrey 36, H. Jupp 34, H. H. Stephenson 41, G. Griffith 86*; James Lillywhite 6-89). The county season began, at noon on a mild Thursday, on as magnificently truthful a wicket as ever cricket was played on. Notwithstanding the early introduction of Mortlock's horrid slows, Sussex made a fast start. Charles Smith was rewarded with a new bat for his 95 [which remained the highest score of his career]. And when the fielding tired, George Wells made 82, for which he received 'talent money', as did John Lillywhite, whose unbeaten 49 contained a five and a six. When not bowling, Mortlock long-stopped in his usual fine form, no bye being scored, although 735 balls were bowled. Surrey's innings could not get far on Friday. Consequent on continuous rain, it was decided at half past four that no play should take place that day, a decision that might have been arrived at a couple of hours earlier, and thus prevented representatives of the press unwillingly idling away their time. There is too much of this kind of thing going on just now. In front of 3,000 Saturday spectators, some creditable scores were made by Surrey. George Griffith's 86 not out earned him talent money, while last man William Mudie's 15 included a fine leg hit for five. The innings closed at 291 – a minority of 37. James Lillywhite's bowling was very good and, with the exception of one change, he was kept on throughout. At about five o'clock, Sussex commenced their second innings, and the batting gained complete mastery. John Lillywhite made 64 in good style, and Mr. Smith again batted well. The stumps were drawn at half past seven, and the match was left drawn.

MIDDLESEX v SUSSEX

At Islington, June 6, 7. **Middlesex won by an innings and 52 runs. ‡Middlesex 261** (T. Case 30, T. Hearne 50, B. B. Cooper 50, J. J. Sewell 35; James Lillywhite 4-123, R. Fillery 3-58); **Sussex 111** (V. E. Walker 9-63) **and 98** (T. Hearne 5-44, V. E. Walker 5-48). The first county match on the new Middlesex Ground, at the Metropolitan Cattle Market, commenced an hour and a half late. Middlesex captain Teddy Walker's insidious twisters were the feature of this contest, his nine wickets in the first innings and five in the second rendering Middlesex's first-day total of 261 sufficient for victory. Sussex were already six down by stumps: five to Mr. Walker's slows, and Charles Payne to a run-out. In the follow-on, Mr. Walker was assisted by Hearne, who also took five wickets, having reached a half-century the previous day, before being caught one-handed by John Lillywhite, who lost his perpendicular in the attempt. Middlesex selected George Wells (who had played for Sussex for 12 years, most recently against Surrey at The Oval two days before this match) because he had spent the first 21 days of his life in Whitechapel, Middlesex. This little hero of doubtful belongings made a single off his first ball, which was in fact the sum total of his earnings in the match.

Teddy Walker's 14 for 111 remained Middlesex's best first-class figures for 24 years, and ensured that the new team, at their new ground, went straight to the top of the county league table – or would have done, had one been thought of in 1864. Of that, more later.

Mr. John Platts, a cattle drover of Alfreton, spent the afternoon playing cricket, but had too much to drink, abused another player, Mr. Strelley, and was sent from the field. He then made his way to the Waggon and Horses where, the ostler said, he "made a great noise, and was more like a wild man than anything". Mr. Strelley arrived, and Mr. Platts offered several times to strike him. Mr. Strelley laughed and said "if you will be quiet, I will pay for a pint of ale for you," to which Mr. Platts replied, "I'll be damned if I have it. I'll have a gallon, and I'll pay for it." Mr. Strelley then "gave him a bit of a shove". Mr. Platts fell down, and Mr. Strelley picked him up and put him in a chair. Twenty-five minutes later, it became clear that Mr. Platts was deceased. Verdict: accidental death. — *Derbyshire Advertiser*, 10 June

Two miles away, at Lord's, things were going from bad to worse. As Walker's men were romping to victory at Islington with the help of several MCC players, MCC themselves were receiving a shoeing from Cambridge University.

At Lord's, June 6, 7. **Cambridge University won by an innings and 88 runs. ‡MCC 81** (E. F. Dyke 4-27, T. F. Fowler 5-37) **and 52** (E. F. Dyke 6-14, T. F. Fowler 3-26); **Cambridge University 221** (T. de Grey 32, A. Walker 53, C. Booth 36, T. F. Fowler 34*; G. Wootton 4-78).

In the absence of almost any player worthy of the nomenclature, MCC fielded a selection of lords, earls and misadventurers. Archibald Smith's sporting pinnacle had been rowing for Cambridge in the 1859 Boat Race (they sank), while Lieutenant Henry Arkwright might have summited Mont Blanc in 1866, had he not been killed by an avalanche on the way up. Two university bowlers – Edwin Dyke and Thomas Fowler – sent down all but two overs, and shared 18 wickets. At one stage during their second innings, MCC were 16 for seven.

The MCC members might have turned to their newspapers for distraction from their shortcomings – but they would not have found it. *Sporting Life* was still at their throats, calling the committee "jealous and irresponsible", and announcing plans for the inaugural assembly of the Cricket Parliament. This, it turned out, was MCC's lowest ebb.

At Lord's, June 9, 10. **MCC won by 63 runs. ‡MCC 110** (W. F. Maitland 8-58) **and 96; Oxford University 99** (S. C. Voules 36; G. Wootton 6-62, J. Grundy 3-22) **and 44** (G. Wootton 4-15, J. Grundy 5-22).

There were certainly no signs of an upturn in MCC's fortunes when they collapsed to 59 for seven on the first day of their game against Oxford University. Their tormentor was William Maitland, a prodigy who represented Oxford in cricket, rackets, the long-jump and quarter-mile (and was later an MP for 20 years). But their professionals came good. Hearne stopped the rot with 26, before Wootton and Grundy twice laid waste to the Oxford batting.

At the end of the game, at the insistence of Charles Marsham – a 35-year-old who had played for MCC at Cambridge and Oxford, but was not in the side at Lord's – an emergency general meeting was held, at which he proposed shortening Law X, to remove any reference to delivery height:

> The ball must be bowled; if thrown or jerked, the umpire must call 'no ball'.

Another player, 31-year-old Henry Perkins, seconded the motion. The MCC committee, and the old guard, insisted that the law should remain as it was. But Frederick Ponsonby, Robert Grimston and George Cavendish – all sons of peers – sprung a surprise by supporting Marsham, and opposition evaporated. Overarm bowling was legalised by 27 votes to 20. The meeting concluded with the good news that Dark and Moses had agreed terms of a lease for Lord's (it took another two years, but the necessary funds were raised). *Sporting Life* was delighted with the law change, calling the decision "good sense", the committee "respectable" and the chairman "noble". And nobody ever mentioned a Cricket Parliament again.

~~

Lord's was a joyous place on Monday 13 June, the day of the Varsity Match. Not even heavy rain, which restricted the morning's attendance to under 100, could disturb the sense of relief around the pavilion. And there was a pleasant surprise.

Ten days earlier, a telegram from George Anderson had announced that Parr's touring team had reached Suez. The canal had not yet been built, so they had to travel across Egypt to Alexandria, before sailing across the Mediterranean. Anderson and Parr had suffered during a rough passage through the Red Sea, but the next leg was even worse: their ship nearly foundered off Italy. The sick and weary Twelve disembarked at Marseille, and completed their journey

> Alfred Shaw and Henry Pendleton, two youths, were each ordered to pay eight shillings for committing wilful damage to grass in a field occupied by Thomas Bell, by playing cricket. — *Derbyshire Times*, 25 June

by land, reaching London on the morning of the Varsity Match. A homesick Caesar went straight back to Godalming, and was met at the station by a group of cheering tradesmen. But Parr, Carpenter, Hayward and Tarrant travelled to Lord's, and received heroes' welcomes. Soon after three, the sun was shining brightly, coaxing 4,000 to the ground.

At Lord's, June 13, 14. **Oxford University won by four wickets. Cambridge University 75** (W. F. Maitland 4-34, A. S. Teape 6-41) **and 136** (A. W. T. Daniel 33, R. D. Balfour 30; W. F. Maitland 4-19); **‡Oxford University 87** (T. S. Curteis 4-23, F. G. Pelham 4-39) **and 125-6** (R. A. H. Mitchell 55*; T. S. Curteis 4-58).

The batsmen struggled on the wet pitch, frequently sliding when running. Despite the delayed start, 20 wickets fell on the opening day: Lyttelton top-scored with 17 for Cambridge; Tritton with 24 for Oxford. Next day, Cambridge lost four wickets before clearing their arrears of 12. The cream of London society turned out, and the attendance swelled to 6,000 as Oxford began a pursuit of 125. Thanks to Mitchell, who hit an unbeaten half-century, they got there at quarter to six, just before the heavens opened again.

The Varsity Match was bookended by contests between the universities and Surrey. Cambridge's game, which ended in a draw, was lit up by 104 from Surrey captain Frederick Burbidge, batting at No. 9. The match was never given first-class status, since Cambridge used 13 players. Oxford were defeated, despite a first-innings lead of 47 and 12 wickets from Maitland. Stephenson twice top-scored for Surrey, and Lockyer surprisingly showed no ill effects from his long sea voyage. He was the only one of Parr's tourists who felt up to playing; the others took a rest, missing the three county matches in mid-June.

NOTTINGHAMSHIRE v KENT

At Nottingham, June 13, 14. **Nottinghamshire won by an innings and 38 runs. ‡Kent 62** (J. Grundy 9-19) **and 124** (J. C. Burton 40; G. Wootton 3-47, A. Shaw 6-31); **Nottinghamshire 224** (C. F. Daft 46, C. Brampton 56, G. Wootton 33; E. Willsher 6-63). Kent, having won the toss, went in first, making only the small score of 62, their innings lasting barely two hours. Grundy bowled throughout, in such exceedingly fine form that nine wickets fell to his credit. Betting was five to one in favour of Nottinghamshire, and by six o'clock they were 52 ahead, with only one wicket down. Charles Daft defied the efforts of the fielders for two hours, before he was tempted out by a slow and stumped. The innings eventually reached 224, an immense majority, though the Kent men looked like making a fight of it when they were 81 for one. But the vision of an even contest was a mirage, the remaining nine wickets falling for the addition of 43.

YORKSHIRE v SURREY

At Sheffield, June 13, 14, 15. **Drawn. ‡Surrey 195** (H. Jupp 41, H. H. Stephenson 46; I. Hodgson 4-62, R. Iddison 3-30) **and 247** (T. Humphrey 74, H. Jupp 110; W. Slinn 4-74, R. Iddison 6-38); **Yorkshire 236** (L. Greenwood 65; T. Sewell 5-79) **and 33-2.** The rain which fell on the previous day put the ground in good condition, and though further showers came during play, the cricketers remained at their posts, so that the inconvenience was trifling. Yorkshire bowled and fielded well, but young Jupp handled his bat remarkably, before his innings was brought to a close by Atkinson, who had to throw himself on the grass to catch the ball. The Surrey innings ended shortly before six o'clock for 195. On Tuesday, in the presence of the most numerous company ever seen at the Bramall Lane ground, Yorkshire found themselves 110 for seven, and the chance of their winning was considered remote. But a change came over the game, and though the Surrey men had frequent consultations, and as frequent changes to the bowling, the Yorkshiremen defied all efforts, scoring 41 more than Surrey. On Wednesday, Jupp and Humphrey, going in first, were together nearly three hours, and put on 159 before they were separated, a partnership believed to be unprecedented at Sheffield. But when Humphrey was at last out, the spell which had so long defied the utmost efforts of the Yorkshiremen was fairly broken, and the Surrey innings closed for 247. Yorkshire had 207 to get to win, and lost two wickets before the stumps were drawn at half-past six.

SUSSEX v KENT

At Hove, June 20, 21. **Sussex won by an innings and 29 runs. ‡Sussex 316** (J. H. Hale 61, G. Wells 69, C. H. Ellis 52, S. A. Leigh 42; E. Willsher 3-111, G. Bennett 3-79); **Kent 177** (W. H. Fryer 65, H. B. Biron 30; James Lillywhite 4-66, H. Stubberfield 4-46) **and 110** (James Lillywhite 5-51). At the conclusion of the first day's play, some reporters observed that the game had afforded further proof of the widely-made assertion that the batting has become too strong for the bowling. The ground was in splendid condition and the weather delightful, though the match started twenty minutes late. James Lillywhite hit too freely before being given out leg before wicket, but in general the bowling was hit about. Stumps were drawn at the conclusion of the Sussex innings. Kent, faced with particularly good bowling (not a wide ball was delivered), fell for 177, and being in a large minority, were again put in. Again Sussex's out-play was capital, and the match ended on the second evening, Kent losing by one innings, and Lillywhite finishing with nine wickets.

The next big events in the calendar were the traditional Gentlemen v Players fixtures: one at The Oval, one at Lord's. The England players were expected to make a glorious return at Lord's, with the exception of Caesar (who had promised to play in a North v South game in Lincolnshire), Clarke (not good enough to be selected), Caffyn and Grace (still in Australia).

Lockyer was already back in action, and Carpenter decided to warm up by appearing for United England at Islington. The opposition captain was Charles Absolon, surely the most prolific bowler never to play first-class cricket. He participated in every game he could find – often twice in a day – and played for 71 years. Only at the age of 50 did he start counting his wickets, racking up 8,500, including 59 hat-tricks, between then and his death at 80. "What makes all this the more remarkable," wrote Wisden's *Almanack*, "is that Mr. Absolon is a welter in weight and a veteran in years".

Despite having 22 players, Absolon's team lost by an innings. He did not bowl himself at all, instead putting his faith in his hired hand, Surrey wicketkeeper Ted Pooley. He took six wickets – including Carpenter for 51 – but made a pair. The morning after the game, the first Gentlemen v Players contest got under way in Kennington.

At The Oval, June 23, 24, 25. **Players won by 205 runs. ‡Players 244** (R. Daft 61, T. Hearne 45*; W. F. Maitland 5-104, G. M. Kelson 4-35) **and 371** (J. Rowbotham 57, H. H. Stephenson 117, W. Mortlock 78; V. E. Walker 4-99); **Gentlemen 201** (F. Burbidge 39, J. Makinson 64*; E. Willsher 3-60, G. Griffith 4-32) **and 209** (C. G. Lyttelton 81, V. E. Walker 47*; G. Wootton 3-58).

The first day was characterised by Mortlock's hitting (he sent one ball so high that three fielders left the catch to each other) and Dick Daft's rapid scoring for the Players. On the second, the crowd were treated to the unfamiliar sight

> Henry and Joseph Edmundson were summoned for playing cricket in Barnes Street on Wednesday. The magistrates said the cricket was becoming very common in the public streets, and the bench were determined to put a stop to so dangerous a practice. — *Preston Chronicle*, 25 June

of one of the Gentlemen, Arthur Daniel, batting with a runner, after being lamed early in his innings. When the Players went in again, Joseph Rowbotham smashed a fifty before he was brilliantly caught by Henry Bull, who ran in many yards and held the ball in his fingertips. Stephenson continued his prime form with a maiden first-class century.

Though Maitland worked hard for his first-innings five-for, and Lyttelton made a composed 81 on the final day, the Gentlemen were beaten. They always were. As anyone leafing through their brand-new *Almanack* could see, the Players had lost only once since 1849 – a streak that included 20 victories. That they would add two more wins in 1864 was a foregone conclusion.

At Lord's, June 27, 28. **Players won by an innings and 68 runs. ‡Players 187** (W. Mortlock 71; W. F. Traill 3-41, H. Arkwright 7-83); **Gentlemen 60** (E. Willsher 4-29, G. F. Tarrant 6-25) **and 59** (E. Willsher 5-26, G. F. Tarrant 5-24).

At Lord's, the involvement of eight of the Australia tourists meant the Gentleman received an even bigger thrashing than usual; only two of them made double figures. Mortlock dominated the Players' innings with a blistering knock, which only ended when Burbidge stuck out his left hand and grabbed a scorcher. Carpenter was cautious in making 20, as was Anderson, but 187 was sufficient for an innings victory, Tarrant and Willsher sharing all the wickets.

Caesar had rather less fun over three rainy days at Sleaford. Playing for the South, he had to contend with the in-form Grundy, and came off second-best.

At Sleaford, June 27, 28, 29. **Drawn. ‡South 99** (J. Grundy 6-42) **and 191** (G. Griffith 61, H. H. Stephenson 31; A. Shaw 4-52, L. Greenwood 3-59); **North 137** (J. Thewlis 77; James Lillywhite 3-57, G. Bennett 5-24) **and 85-5** (G. Bennett 3-36).

The pitch was green, the breeze stiff, and run-making difficult. The South's 99 spanned 76 overs, and the only batter who rose to the occasion was John Thewlis, who made more than half the North's runs. An interesting finish was in prospect, with the North half out chasing 153, when the weather closed in, sending everyone home in a sulk. Caesar and Stephenson, among others, had an damp overnight trip to London, for an exhibition match at The Oval.

Pitting together the amateurs and professionals of the south, the game was a disappointment for Caesar, who made seven, but kept Stephenson in form with a handsome 58. Willsher also padded his stats, with nine for 50 from 46 overs, as the professionals won by an innings. At the same time, in Nottingham, the best players of the north were enjoying a much closer contest.

NOTTINGHAMSHIRE v YORKSHIRE

At Nottingham, June 30, July 1, 2. **Yorkshire won by 99 runs. ‡Yorkshire 125** (J. Berry 39; G. Wootton 4-37) **and 236** (B. W. Waud 42, G. Anderson 99*; J. Grundy 3-62, J. Jackson 3-44); **Nottinghamshire 124** (G. Parr 35; W. Slinn 6-19) **and 138** (W. Oscroft 31, G. Parr 34; W. Slinn 6-34). Splendid bowling, first-rate batting, scientific defence and good fielding characterised the play, and the size of the crowd gave satisfactory proofs of cricket's popularity in Nottingham. One of the principal features of the match was the presence of several of the Australian twelve: Anderson, Parr and Tinley were all greeted with applause. Yorkshire batted first, and were 124 for six when Anderson hit the ball back tremendously fast to Wootton, who found it too hot to hold. No matter: he had him caught at cover point next over, and only one more run was added. It has of late been considered by many admirers of the game that Parr, the Nottinghamshire captain, was getting past cricket, but these must have been agreeably surprised at the revival of his old form. William Slinn ended his magnificent innings of 35, and finished with six wickets for 19 runs. Yorkshire batted again with a deficit of one, and six were out for 72. But Anderson proved frightfully troublesome to the Nottinghamshire bowlers, and reached 99 with a single off Grundy, who then bowled Slinn, the last man, and Anderson's chance of a county hundred was dashed. Nottinghamshire had 237 runs to get off, but were out for 138, Slinn dismissing another six men.

By now, county cricket was in full swing. The Llanelli Railway Company stopped their trains between stations so that passengers could alight and watch Carmarthenshire (97 and 86) play Breconshire (139 and 44 for two) at Dolgarreg. The gentlemen of Cheshire and Shropshire, meanwhile, had to contend with what *Eddowes's Shrewsbury Journal* called "atmospheric influences".

> We do not know whether the Cheshire players had invoked the gods to witness their progress, but it is certain that the applauding thunders were very loud, and the odds and ends of showers were very damping to the spirits of Salop. The amount of rain was not so great, but the hail was very large, and one fielder was observed to hurl a lump of ice into the nape of his neighbour's neck, thinking he was putting down

> the wicket with the ball. The effect of the weather was also apparent in one of the Shropshire players walking from his wickets without any assignable cause. The game was drawn.

At Battersea Park, on their newly spruced-up, fenced-off ground, the Civil Service beat a House of Commons team brimming with political talent. The Commons captain, Charles Carnegie (Liberal, Forfarshire), was one of only three to reach double figures, and they followed on, despite the participation of Charles Fitzwilliam (Liberal, Malton), a first-class cricketer. Other failures included Augustus Anson (Liberal, Lichfield), who had won the Victoria Cross during the Indian Mutiny, Charles du Cane (Conservative, Maldon), later Governor of Tasmania, and Charles Henry Rolle Hepburn-Stuart-Forbes-Trefusis (Conservative, Devon North), later Under-Secretary of State for India.

Newspaper columns were brimming with amusing and acrimonious incidents from the village green. The *Preston Herald* reported that, in Lancashire, Rawtenstall were one run from victory when they lost their ninth wicket, and discovered that their last man, Thomas Wood, had gone home. The same paper, reporting on a married versus single match at Chorley, observed that: "If the superior advantages of the married state, about which we hear so much, may be considered as fairly tested by a game of cricket, the result will have a telling effect in favour of celibacy."

Some correspondents, regardless of the newspaper or importance of the game, seemed determined to have a whinge:

> The match took place on Saturday 4 June, on the beautiful ground at Llangattock Park, where cricket is permitted by His Grace the Duke of Beaufort, whose generosity is cherished with the heartiest feelings of pleasure – feelings which would continue to flow in an uninterrupted stream if it were not for the all too frequent obnoxious display of "a little brief authority" by several pretentious mechanical subordinates.

Six young boys were charged with stealing an ash plank from a barn on Sunday 12 June. It appeared that they had taken it for the purpose of making cricket stumps. As Mr. Cropper did not wish to press the case against them, they were discharged with a reprimand. — *Kendal Mercury*, 25 June

> Abergavenny scored 146, and Crickhowell made 147, with six wickets to go down. — *Cambria Daily Leader*

> The encounter between Wye and Mersham was played on Wye's notorious field, and finished with a general thanksgiving that no fatal casualty occurred. Much credit is due to the active attendance of the people of the district, who were ready to assist the wounded of either side. The scores were very small, but after lunch each cricketer made his will, and British pluck showed itself. Mr. Hornby's last will and testament contained a codicil bequeathing a roller and water pot to the Wye Cricket Club, but it is hoped that the Club will not wait until his demise before procuring those articles. — *Canterbury Journal*

> The report of the match between Fulbourn and Swaffham Prior is made out in such an unintelligible and careless manner that we cannot insert it. — *Cambridge Chronicle and Journal*

> The first innings was closely contested, but the bowling of Longfield and Foot proved too much for the North Cork Militia in their second, and left the victory to Newberry by 29 runs. Although the weather was most auspicious, it is to be regretted that the fair sex did not more numerously favour the players with their presence. — *Cork Constitution*

In the Bristol newspapers, two clubs carried on a dispute which lasted throughout June. After challenging Redcliffe to a game with two weeks' notice, Stoke Bishop withdrew at one o'clock on the day of the match – half an hour before the start – because they could not muster a team. Having gone to the expense of preparing the ground, the Redcliffe secretary was apoplectic. "I think it is right to let the cricketers of Bristol know what treatment they may be likely to receive at the hands of the Stoke Bishop Club," he wrote.

The Stoke Bishop captain, F. B. Budge, penned an acid reply: "I regret that the secretary of the Redcliffe Cricket Club should have so far forgotten himself as to trouble the public with what is entirely a private matter, and one which should have been set at rest by the letter of apology I addressed to him. The course he has subsequently adopted proves that it is possible to be too courteous toward persons with whom you are imperfectly acquainted."

Various Stoke Bishop members weighed in. "The Redcliffe secretary, never having forgiven the last season's thrashings, was determined that his club should beat Stoke Bishop this year," wrote one. "Mr. Budge declined, with thanks." Another added: "It was out of the question for us to play, not least since Redcliffe had engaged the services of two or three first-rate cricketers. When one of our members turned up at the ground, the Redcliffe secretary was present, and offered him an insult, the use of which will from now on cause him to be regarded in his proper light by the members of Stoke Bishop Cricket Club. In conclusion, I think the name of the Stoke Bishop club is too well established to fear the assaults of the Redcliffe secretary."

The Redcliffe secretary, though, was determined to have the last word. "No one will attempt to dispute that the name of the Stoke Bishop club is well established," he wrote. "For although it has not figured to any extraordinary extent in the columns devoted to cricket, it has certainly occupied a very conspicuous position in the police reports."

Elsewhere, umpiring was a common cause of argument. A game in Suffolk, between Lidgate and Cavendish, descended into rancour owing to what the *Bury and Norwich Post* described as "the discourteous and disagreeable conduct of the Cavendish umpire". A letter promptly arrived blaming Lidgate.

> Dear Sir — One of the Lidgate gentlemen came to the Cavendish umpire and asked him to lend them the ball to practise with. This, being contrary to the game, the umpire did not feel disposed to do, there being several others available. This offended them, and from that time they were continually trying to get up something to annoy him.

Another set-to occurred in Cumberland, though the *Whitehaven News* was keen to gloss over it: Maryport reached 164 thanks to the batting of two

> Last night Henry Trumper, a rough fellow, well known to the police, who was the worse for liquor, was in the cricket field demanding pennies from the boys. As they refused to give him any, he became abusive and violent, ran after them, and attempted to strike them. Not succeeding in that, he took one of the stumps and, throwing it with all his force, struck one of the boys on the head. The stump was broken with the force of the blow. The prisoner was very violent on the way to the police station. In his defence, he said that he was sorry for what he had done, but he was so drunk that he really did not know what he was about. The magistrate ordered a fine of £3, or imprisonment with hard labour for two months. — *London Evening Standard*, 29 June

brothers, Miles and Thomas Tickle, and when Whitehaven had reached 47 for three, "an unfortunate circumstance occurred which put an end to the match". The *Cumberland Paquet* was less cryptic, reporting two versions of events. The Whitehaven players said their umpire had immediately turned down a run-out appeal, but Maryport claimed he had initially said "out", only to retract his decision under pressure from the batsman. The two accounts agreed on one thing, which was that the Maryport players quit the game in disgust.

Perhaps unsurprisingly, lbw decisions caused the most dissent, and the previous year's fiddling with the law did not help. Few, it seemed, could remember whether the ball still had to pitch in line with the wickets, if that requirement had now been removed, or if that removal had been overturned. Unhappy batsmen took advantage of the uncertainty to dispute their dismissals. The *Sheffield Independent* reported a typical incident.

> Two clubs were playing a cricket match, not a dozen miles from the city. The second side was getting its second innings, and in danger of losing. The umpire at the wicket gave one of their men out for leg before wicket; he refused to go out, and his friends on the edge of the field called to him to stay where he was. The umpire, while maintaining that his decision was correct, was too timid to enforce it.
>
> A little afterwards, the last man was in, and five runs were wanted to win, when the umpire gave him out, caught. Emboldened by the previous man's success, he also refused to go, and the umpire again failed to enforce his decision. The umpire afterwards explained that he expected, from what he knew about the team's conduct formerly, that had he enforced his decision, the team would have started a fist-fight.

Reports of this kind were an almost weekly occurrence in 1864, and rather dampen the modern-day desire to portray Victorian cricket as an almost unrecognisably genteel game. On 25 June, *Field* took a philosophical position:

> Who has *ever* been out leg before wicket? We have seen scores of men retire from the wicket with a gloomy brow, and in sullen silence. So it will always be. Let them unbosom themselves to their own side in the tent, or to their wives and daughters, who form a willing and believing audience. If the umpire thinks it is out, what is the use of disputing it? Exit at once, for the sake of example. Talk the matter over afterwards. Enlist as much sympathy, especially from the women, as possible.

> Congratulate yourself on what you would have done, but for having been given out unfairly. But do not imagine for one moment that any alteration to Law 24 will make the slightest difference to your disgust.

One of the greatest umpire-bullies of the age, Teddy Grace, had not yet returned from Australia, so his stamping ground – the West Country, and particularly the Lansdown, South Wales and West Gloucestershire clubs – must have been relatively quiet during the spring. In his absence, his eldest brother, Henry, had agreed to take over the organisation of the main event of the Lansdown season: the visit of All England on the last day of June. Lansdown, of course, would be allowed 22 players, but even so, the visiting line-up looked unbeateable: John Lillywhite, Humphrey, Tarrant, Tom Hayward and his brother Daniel, Pooley, Carpenter, Thomas Bignall of Nottinghamshire, Hearne, and the Yorkshire all-rounder Billy Goodhew. All England were certain to win. There was just one snag: they were a man short.

Someone then remembered their last match at Bristol, at the end of the 1863 season. Teddy and Henry Grace had been in the home team, as had a younger brother. He was only a child, but he had done all right. Perhaps he might be invited to make up the numbers?

JULY

Nobody called him "W. G." as a teenager. They called him "Gilbert" – if they noticed him at all. Why would they, with Teddy on the scene? On 19 July 1860, opening the batting for West Gloucestershire, Teddy had scored a rapid, chanceless 150, and captured the attention of the nation. He was just 18. Over the next three seasons, his feats were prodigious. Guesting for MCC against the Gentlemen of Kent during Canterbury Week in August 1862, he claimed five for 77, carried his bat for 192, then took all ten wickets in the Kent second innings. A year later, he hit 112 in a Gentlemen of the South total of 193 at Southampton; the next-highest score was 16. The newspapers were now reporting his every cricketing move (and several of his non-cricketing moves, such as his possible romantic interests), and he joined Parr's Australia tour as a hero. Teddy routinely outperformed his older brothers, Henry and Alfred. This 1860 scorecard – which also includes their father, Henry senior – is typical.

WEST GLOUCESTERSHIRE

E. M. Grace b Housin	150
A. Pocock b Daubeny	44
A. Grace b Housin	2
H. Grace, jr. run out	10
Bramhall lbw b Housin	1
Westwood b Belcher	25
Kelly c Homfray b Gruning	36
Metcalf run out	14
W. G. Grace b Daubeny	51
H. Pocock b Daubeny	4
H. Grace, sr. not out	0
Extras	44
Total	**381**

Gilbert, batting at number nine, was quite forgotten. Though he was a good round-arm bowler, this was his first fifty – completed four days after his twelfth birthday – and a rare batting triumph. He had never previously made more than 13, and did not score another half-century against proper opposition for three years.

The 1863 season began badly for Gilbert, in all senses. Convalescing after bout of pneumonia – potentially fatal for a thin 14-year-old – he played for a Lansdown XXII against All England. This was his first taste of top-quality bowling and, batting at No. 15 and No. 14, he was twice dismissed by Tinley for nought. He made another pair later in the season, with Teddy the bowler in both innings. Then runs started to come: 86 against Clifton, 74 against Stoke Bishop, and an unbeaten 52 against Gentlemen of Somerset in August. But it was an innings of 32, when Bristol faced All England the following week, that stuck in the mind. Gilbert certainly remembered it well: in his 1891 autobiography, he wrote that it was his "first match against first-class professional bowling" (he had evidently forgotten his double-failure in the spring). And though the All England bowlers were Jackson, Tinley, Willsher, Tarrant and Hayward – the same quintet that had bested Lansdown in May – Bristol won by an innings.

Gilbert accepted the offer to make up the numbers in the All England side for their match against Lansdown, beginning on 30 June 1864. He had played five matches in the season, for Hanham, Clifton and Stapleton, and had accumulated 115 runs at an average of 23, and 29 wickets. He did not bowl for All England, though. "I batted sixth man, which I considered rather a high compliment in so strong a team," he wrote. "I was in for over half an hour while I made 15. Just when I got set, an unfortunate mistake of John Lillywhite's caused me to be run out. But I did not mind that."

After one more game, for Clifton against Lansdown, Gilbert was approached by Henry with an exciting proposal. South Wales, a club for whom

Dr. William Webber, of Mount Sion, Tunbridge Wells, complained that the Town Council had allowed a drain near his home to be left exposed, and that as a result some of his patients had contracted fevers, and one had died. Rumours abounded that typhus and scarlet fever were spreading, and many people left the town. A health inspector found no cause for concern, and concluded that the dead man had remained too long in damp clothes while umpiring a cricket match on a rainy day. On Saturday 2 July, a thousand traders, furious at a reduction in business, descended on Dr. Webber's house to yell insults, let off fireworks, throw potatoes at the windows, and burn a straw effigy of Dr. Webber in the form of a pig. — *Sussex Advertiser*, 13 September

Henry and Teddy occasionally played, were about to depart on their annual tour of south-east England – but there wasn't yet any sign of Teddy. Could Gilbert stand in for him, until he returned from Australia? This meant games against Surrey at the Oval, and against the Gentlemen of Sussex at Hove.

Of course, Gilbert's answer was yes. A warm-up game at Sevenoaks – his first appearance outside the Bristol area – yielded five runs and 13 wickets, and the brothers were in high spirits when they arrived at The Oval on the morning of 11 July. Their mood was dampened almost immediately. The South Wales captain, John Lloyd, told Henry that the Sussex team, for the second game, was expected to be very strong. Furthermore, Lloyd had heard that Teddy would be back in time to play at Hove, so planned to drop Gilbert. Henry's response was forthright: "The boy was asked to play in both matches, and he shall play in both or none." It was agreed that Gilbert would play at Hove – in Henry's place.

> Surrey won the toss for choice of innings, and at half-past twelve Messrs. Collier and Calvert went in, to the bowling of H. Grace and W. E. Grace. Mr. Calvert drove H. Grace in the first over for 4, and then in the third over for 6. Mr. Collier scored 2 and was caught by Mr. Lloyd (the wicketkeeper), bowled W. E. Grace. — *Evening Standard*

This, then, was how W. G. Grace was introduced to the wider cricketing public. The following day, the *Evening Standard* got his initials right (as did the *Morning Advertiser* and *Globe*) and reported that he had taken four first-innings wickets before being bowled for five. South Wales followed on, and Gilbert managed 38 second time round, then added another wicket to his tally before Surrey eased to victory. But he received no further mention in the papers.

On the first morning of the Hove fixture, Thursday 14 July, Gilbert was feeling the pressure. "After the discussion between Henry and the South Wales captain, I was eager to do well," he recalled. "Henry was not playing, and I felt that the entire responsibility of the family credit was resting on my shoulders. Up to the last moment, we hoped Teddy would turn up – and I desired it eagerly, to give me heart. His ringing voice and cheery tones would have been invaluable to me." Teddy did not arrive – South Wales began the game with ten men – but by six o'clock that evening, his absence had been rendered irrelevant.

SOUTH WALES

Calvert b Burnett	9
Lloyd b Horwood	82
W. G. Grace b Pratt	170
F. Price c Pratt b Ravenhill	7
Bishop b Horwood	1
W. Price c Brand b Ravenhill	1
Kennedy b Pratt	46
Hartnell b Napper	23
Homfray b Napper	4
Jones not out	0
E. M. Grace absent	
Extras	15
Total	**358**

The *Sporting Gazette* called Gilbert's 170 "the finest innings played on the ground this season". *Bell's Life* said it was a chanceless hundred, and *Sporting Life* simply called it "brilliant". The most fulsome praise came from the *Brighton Gazette*: "The Welsh gentlemen expected great things of Mr. Grace – and were not disappointed. He completely put our Sussex gentlemen hors de combat, sending the ball about in every direction, with the exception of leg hits, scarcely any of which he made … he obtained the enormous score of 170. He was followed by numbers to the pavilion, amidst the loudest cheers."

Teddy arrived in London just as the Friday morning newspapers were hitting the stands. On learning of his brother's innings, he decided he would be surplus to requirements at Hove, and went home to Bristol. Sussex followed

John Gillat, an omnibus conductor, said that on Saturday night he had a dispute with a passenger, William Burgh, aged 21, about the fare from the Brecknock Arms to Edward Street in Marylebone, London. Mr. Burgh, a painter, took hold of Mr. Gillat's arm, then struck him a tremendous blow on the right eye with a cricket bat, saying "damn you, take that". Mr. Burgh ran off, but was stopped and given into custody. The prisoner was bailed for £120. — *The Sun*, 4 July. *Burgh was later sentenced to nine months' hard labour.*

on 208 behind, and the game ended with South Wales five wickets down, and 16 short of victory. Gilbert, second time round, was unbeaten on 56. Two days later, he celebrated his 16th birthday.

Gilbert was now undroppable. After another low-key game at Sevenoaks (where he kept wicket), he made his first appearance at Lord's, for South Wales against MCC. The newsmen focused on the return of Teddy, but he marked the occasion with a duck, while Gilbert made 50. He had quiet games at Islington and Southgate, but concluded the tour with 34 and 47 against I Zingari at Lord's. The following day, having returned home, he struck 15 and 78 for Hanham against Weston-super-Mare. A new Grace had arrived.

~~

July was when the 1864 county contests really heated up: there were six before, and six after, but 12 in the month itself. The July games established Surrey and Cambridgeshire as the frontrunners, with Middlesex just behind, Nottinghamshire, Sussex and Yorkshire somewhere in the middle, and Hampshire and Kent the backmarkers. Surrey's batting was proving indomitable – as was Cambridgeshire's bowling.

CAMBRIDGESHIRE v YORKSHIRE

At Cambridge, July 4, 5. **Cambridgeshire won by three wickets. ‡Yorkshire 114** (G. F. Tarrant 5-46) **and 152** (G. Anderson 42, L. Greenwood 59; G. F. Tarrant 4-56, T. Hayward 6-72); **Cambridgeshire 144** (J. Smith 31, T. Hayward 39, R. P. Carpenter 44*; I. Hodgson 4-61) **and 125-7** (F. C. Pryor 64; G. R. Atkinson 3-40). After their victory at Nottingham, the Yorkshire team were invited to Cambridge to commemorate the return of the three Cambridge players, Carpenter, Hayward and Tarrant. The Yorkshiremen were looked on as great guns – and well they might have been, but not here. Tarrant swept them aside for 114. When Cambridge batted, Hayward and Carpenter hit smartly, the innings reaching 144, though Carpenter was unable to finish, having been severely hit upon the fingers. Yorkshire in the second innings were more fortunate. Luke Greenwood made 56, and Anderson 42 by excellent play. Cambridgeshire were left 123 to get. This they accomplished, owing to the splendid batting of the 19-year-old colt, Frederick Pryor.

SURREY v NOTTINGHAMSHIRE

At The Oval, July 4, 5, 6. **Surrey won by ten wickets. ‡Surrey 468** (T. Humphrey 75, W. Mortlock 48, H. H. Stephenson 119, E. Dowson 43, T. Lockyer 108*; J. Jackson 3-98) **and 4-0; Nottinghamshire 283** (R. Daft 56, T. Bignall 49, A. Shaw 64; G. Griffith 3-113, W. Mortlock 5-82) **and 188** (C. Brampton 82; T. Lockyer 6-44). On the first day, there was some big play. Stephenson, the all-rounder, and Lockyer, the wicketkeeper, gained complete mastery over the bowling, commencing a regular leather-driving business. Drives and leg hits followed each other rapidly, and both men scored hundreds. The Nottinghamshire side, after a hard day's fagging, looked almost beat. When they batted, the sharp-shooting of Griffith and the slows of Mortlock put them in even more trouble. Several, by severe blows and wounds, were not up to their work. They finished in a minority of 185, and consequently were obliged to follow their innings. Charles Brampton, though suffering from illness (a man being allowed to run for him) batted in good style, marking 82 against various changes of bowling, and deservedly received talent money. Lockyer, having relinquished the gloves, was very effective, gaining six wickets. The innings closed for 188, leaving Surrey four runs to get, which they obtained without losing a wicket. It was an extraordinary run-getting match, no less than 939 being scored in total.

Six counties had now registered one win. The exceptions were Kent, who had lost both their games, and Hampshire, who had yet to play. Their first-class match at Southampton in the second week of July 1864 was their first since the founding of the modern club, at the Antelope Inn, on 12 August the previous year. Teams called Hampshire had been taking the field since the mid-eighteenth century, but the new organisation owed its conception to a cabal of retired cricketers, including Thomas Chamberlayne, once High Sheriff of Hampshire; Sir Frederick Hutchison Hervey-Bathurst, a former MCC president; and Daniel Day, who established the cricket field at the inn. To call the game Hampshire's first would be misleading, and that is probably just as well, since they were thrashed.

HAMPSHIRE v SUSSEX

At Southampton, July 7, 8. **Sussex won by ten wickets. ‡Hampshire 63** (James Lillywhite 5-22, C. H. Ellis 4-40) **and 122** (G. H. Case 48; James Lillywhite 5-58, C. H. Ellis 3-31); **Sussex 185** (C. H. Smith 47, R. Fillery 35) **and 1-0.** This was a one-sided affair. It was generally thought that it would have filled the three days allotted, but cricket meets with many changes, and this match was brought to close in half that time, even though the Brighton train arrived late, delaying the start. Hampshire won at the first event, viz. the toss, and decided to bat, but that was the only luck they met with. Something of a funk was soon established, and the wickets fell so fast that there really was nothing worth recording. Hampshire only placed on the score 63 runs in the first innings. George Case could not bat, since he had arrived at the ground after the pitch had been rolled. This was a great loss, as in the next innings he contributed 48 in splendid style. The united score of both innings of Hampshire amounted to 185, just matching the Sussex first innings, and they needed only one to win.

It did not help Hampshire's prospects that Sussex brought six professionals. Hampshire were mostly amateurs, and their best batsman, John St. John Frederick – who had hit a century in the match immediately preceding this – was absent, having accepted an invitation to play for MCC at Lord's. Kent, meanwhile, were heading for their third successive defeat.

KENT v SURREY

At Gravesend, July 7, 8. **Surrey won by eight wickets. ‡Kent 94** (G. Griffith 3-34, T. Sewell 5-12) **and 177** (G. M. Kelson 80, M. A. Troughton 35; G. Griffith 6-57); **Surrey 246** (W. Mortlock 82, H. H. Stephenson 63; E. Willsher 3-72, F. Norley 5-52) **and 29-2.** Kent won the toss and batted, but Sewell was on the spot and bowling splendidly, and the innings lasted a little under two hours. Further play was deferred until after dinner, and when Stephenson joined Mortlock at 45 for three, the Kent team had a rare treat at leather hunting, the batsmen hitting away whenever they had a chance. The tide was set in favour of Surrey, their two batsmen putting on 129. Surrey closed for 246, being 152 in advance of Kent. George Kelson made some of the best batting during the whole match, departing with 80, including ten fours splendidly got. The Kent second innings reached 177, leaving only 25 for Surrey to get. The winning hit was an on-drive for four, and there was a race for the ball, which Mr. Kelson succeeded in getting.

Kent's miserable season continued at Lord's, where they were soundly beaten by an England eleven, despite being allowed 13 players. The match was a personal success for their opening batsman Harry Fryer, but not in the manner expected. Until 1863, he had been Kent's wicketkeeper, but had fallen from a cart and lost an eye. Now, he scored 11 and two, but claimed career-best figures of eight for 40 on the opening day, sweeping aside the cream of English batting – despite woeful fielding from his team-mates.

July was a tough month for several of the weaker counties. At Birkenhead, Shropshire were forced to spend an entire day in the field – a rare phenomenon in the north of England – while the batsmen put on 307. Across the Mersey, Cheshire had a similar experience at Liverpool, who ran up 334, with Fred Crooke making 142. Norfolk put on two horror shows against MCC, home and away: chasing 192 at Lord's, they were bundled out for 20, and having earned a slender first-innings lead at East Dereham, they capitulated for 37.

Northumberland, perhaps the strongest county not yet playing first-class cricket, had the best of a draw against Stockton-on-Tees, a match memorable less for the play than for a remarkable epistolary spat it triggered. The fuse was set by 'Elfin', the opinionated cricket correspondent of the *Newcastle Daily Chronicle*.

> A one-sided cricket match is never a very interesting exhibition, and this was an unsatisfactory contest. It is not usual to play proper cricket on the brow of an irregular hill, or in a region scattered with lumps, stones and broken bottles. Northumberland possess the worst ground in the north – worse even than Kelso, which is saying a great deal. Furthermore, it is contrary to both the law and practice of cricket to roll a pitch without the express permission of the umpires, but Northumberland did so prior to commencing their second innings.

The Northumberland officials were outraged, and sent an indignant letter to the *Chronicle*, which refused to include it in their next edition, writing instead: "Any proper explanation we would have been glad to publish, but we decline printing the very offensive letter you have sent us." A rival newspaper, the *Newcastle Journal*, published it instead.

> Dear sir — Allow us to explain our apparent indiscretion, for which we have been so mercilessly abused by your reporter, Elfin. The man whom we employ to look after the ground has directions always to roll after rain, and accordingly in the morning he put the roller all over the ground before any of us arrived, or of course we should have prevented him from doing so. This was explained to the Stockton men, and they understood it at once. The *Chronicle* is doing everything in its power to run down our club.

Matters came to a head during a fixture between Tynemouth and Middlesbrough, which involved several Northumberland players. The arrival of Elfin, said the *Chronicle*, had not been met with a warm reception.

> Our reporter was favoured with a volley of low abuse from one of the blackguards among the Tynemouth players. We shall seek an apology, but should this be refused, we shall protect our staff by expunging from our columns all reports of cricket matches other than those which are respectable and well conducted.

No apology was forthcoming but, at the request of the Middlesbrough team – who won by nine wickets – the *Chronicle* relented, and published the scores. The *Journal*, of course, took great joy in continuing to publish letters bashing Elfin.

> Dear sir — Elfin began his match report by writing: "A one-sided cricket match is never a very interesting exhibition." I think the words apply with equal force to any report the *Chronicle* may write. It matters not how well the Northumberland team bat, it is all "flukes" and "unworthy skillessness" (what that means your readers can tell no more than I). As for the description Elfin gives of the Northumberland ground, I can only write that the labourer who prepares the ground must be forgiven, for he knows as little about cricket as Elfin does.

The mid-July batch of county fixtures brought wickets galore: two matches were over in two days. Middlesex and Cambridgeshire joined Surrey and Sussex on two wins, while Hampshire and Yorkshire each suffered a second defeat. With Middlesex sticking to Islington (where victory was set up by Bransby Cooper, who later moved to Australia and played in the first Test), Cambridgeshire made a home at Lord's, where Tarrant caused havoc on the minefield.

MIDDLESEX v HAMPSHIRE

At Islington, July 11, 12. **Middlesex won by an innings and 38 runs. ‡Hampshire 114** (T. Hearne 3-55, W. Catling 5-29) **and 93** (T. Hearne 4-43, W. Catling 3-28); **Middlesex 245** (E. W. Tritton 49, B. B. Cooper 89; F. Walton 3-48). Hampshire accrued runs by steady accumulation, until Mr. Frederick arrived at the fall of the first wicket, and hit up a rapid 29. But he was caught and bowled off William Catling, who then found Henry

Maturin's timber yard. Several others succumbed to Catling, and Hampshire were all out for 114. When Middlesex batted, run-getting was the order of the day, and the bowling was several times changed to no effect. Mr. Cooper made 89 without giving a chance, and in departing was greeted with rounds of applause. In the second innings, it was soon evident that Hampshire would not have a shadow of a chance, Mr. Maturin being the only one to make a stand, that gentleman scoring 28, to add to his first innings 23, by some splendid cricket.

CAMBRIDGESHIRE v NOTTINGHAMSHIRE

At Lord's, July 18, 19. **Cambridgeshire won by 18 runs. ‡Cambridgeshire 122** (D. Hayward 37; J. Grundy 3-15, R. C. Tinley 6-49) **and 113** (T. Hayward 40; J. Grundy 5-36, R. C. Tinley 5-51); **Nottinghamshire 59** (G. F. Tarrant 7-30, F. R. Reynolds 3-25) **and 158** (J. Jackson 36; G. F. Tarrant 3-69, F. R. Reynolds 4-39, T. Hayward 3-23). Nottinghamshire's fielding was good and lively, and Cambridgeshire were got rid of for 122, but the score of Nottinghamshire is soon recorded, for it only amounted to 59. During the innings, Dick Daft was severely hurt by a ball from Frederick Reynolds, which caused him to retire for a time. At the end of the first day, Cambridgeshire, in their second innings, had 55 for four wickets. In the morning they made it up to 113, and Nottinghamshire needed 177 to win. Every run gained was cheered, and although Nottinghamshire lost, it was one of the best contested matches that have taken place this season.

The next game pitted Sussex against Surrey – a key contest, since they were the only teams with two wins. It was a close one, too, until Caesar marched out at No. 7 to play the greatest innings of his life. Surrey only had to bat once, though James Lillywhite put in a Herculean effort with the ball, taking six for 154 from 101 overs.

SUSSEX v SURREY

At Hove, July 18, 19, 20. **Surrey won by an innings and 54 runs. ‡Sussex 213** (C. H. Ellis 54, H. Stubberfield 40; W. Mortlock 3-53, G. Griffith 4-41) **and 152** (C. H. Smith 33, G. Wells 30; W. Shepherd 8-49); **Surrey 419** (T. Humphrey 60, H. Jupp 71, W. Mortlock 69, J. Caesar 132*, J. Street 31; James Lillywhite 6-154). Sussex on the first day made 213, of which number Charles Ellis contributed 54 by a display of some very admirable batting, and Henry Stubberfield (the last man in) rather surprised even his admirers by augmenting the total by 40, the highest score of his life. Sussex seemed to have a goodly total until the Surrey colts, Humphrey and Jupp, hit their straps, taking the total to 113 without giving a ghost of a chance. Five wickets quickly fell on the second morning, rendering the balance of the match uncertain, but Caesar made the astonishing score of 132, carrying out his bat. Stumps were drawn when the Surrey innings closed at 419. Sussex had 206 to go in against, but only succeeded in scoring 152. Mortlock made a magnificent catch off James Lillywhite, the ball being struck a tremendous height in the air. Mr. Smith made his apologies for the duck's egg he obtained in the first innings, by a very respectable 33 in the second, but despite all their efforts Sussex were sorely worsted.

KENT v NOTTINGHAMSHIRE

At Crystal Palace, July 21, 22, 23. **Nottinghamshire won by 74 runs. ‡Nottinghamshire 143** (G. Wootton 38; E. Willsher 4-51, W. H. Fryer 3-47) **and 165** (R. Daft 78, T. Bignall 41; E. Willsher 5-53, F. Norley 3-52); **Kent 124** (W. McCanlis 38; J. Grundy 7-53) **and 110** (W. Oscroft 4-17). The cricket ground attached to the Crystal Palace, on account of its recent construction, was not in a very good condition, being rather lumpy. Nottinghamshire batted first, and the innings terminated for 143, but when stumps were drawn at seven o'clock, Kent had lost seven wickets for 80. The next morning, thanks to the completion of Grundy's seven-wicket harvest, Nottinghamshire were soon batting again, and Dick Daft, much recovered from his injury at Lord's, hit a grand 78, in the face of some very creditable fielding. Kent needed 184 to win, and were 43 for four overnight. William McCanlis batted well for the second time in the match, but Nottinghamshire were victorious.

This was the first first-class game – indeed, the first match of any decent standard – at Crystal Palace. After the Palace was relocated to Norwood, south of London, in 1854, pleasure gardens were laid out to the east. Benjamin Waterhouse Hawkins's life-sized dinosaur models were the first attraction to be installed, and by 1864 there were fountains, a pneumatic railway and a handsome sports ground, home of the Crystal Palace cricket and football clubs. In the hope of attracting prestigious teams, the Crystal Palace Company spent the early months of the year draining and re-turfing the ground.

Securing the Kent fixture was a coup, and for a time there was speculation that Crystal Palace might become the capital's third major cricket ground – even that it might one day be the best (on the first Test tour of England, in 1882, the Australians played three games at Crystal Palace, and did not visit Lord's at all). But distance from central London remained a major obstacle, and such ambition came to naught long before the Palace burned down in 1936.

Lord's geared up for its 1864 showpiece event, Eton v Harrow, with a match pitting the Lords and Commons against I Zingari, the strongest gentlemen's wandering team of the time. Only by fielding 22 players could the politicians compete on anything like level terms.

The following day, thousands of the finest in English society descended on the ground to watch Eton play Harrow. As always, a number of news correspondents were in awe of their betters. The *Daily News* was typical.

> If a foreigner had stood yesterday afternoon in any thoroughfares leading to St John's Wood, he must have speedily learned that some peculiar festival was in course of celebration: the placards on the omnibuses, the ribbons, the parasols, the steadiness with which the traffic converged to a centre, the joyous holiday look on the ladies and gentlemen, the wholly aristocratic aspect of the handsome boys.
>
> Once in the ground, the distinctive characteristics of the mass of people looking on were fully apparent. There were of course no poor, not a single figure whose appearance bespoke aught but plenitude of means. Hampers were unpacked, lunch eaten and wine quaffed.
>
> There was no boisterous demonstration, and it is necessary to insist on this, as the newspapers reported that some very unfair strictures were passed upon the spectators. *The Times* accused them of "an excessive license of chaffing" and "bawling out for the very purpose of balking a player" and of being "ungenerous and unchivalrous in the highest degree". The noisiest demonstration of the day came on the Prince and Princess of Wales driving into the enclosure at four o'clock. Harrow made 242; Eton made 63 and 112.

In truth, Eton v Harrow *did* bring out the worst in the schoolboys – not during the game, but in the streets and hostelries of London afterwards. In 1856, the headmaster of Eton had decided the trip was not worth the trouble, and the fixture took place at Harrow. More than once, MCC considered refusing

On Friday, at the Police Court, a youth named Hales was charged with stealing a cricket bat from Willenhall Cricket Club. Mr. Bennett, the club captain, said that on the back of the bat there were two circles, in which the name "Willenhall" was stamped. On the bat being produced, the varnish had been scraped off where the stamps were said to have been. The prisoner was committed to trial at the Sessions. — *Wolverhampton Chronicle*, 6 July the use of Lord's. For the 1864 match, they insisted on a strong police presence. This precaution was considered beyond the pale by one correspondent to the *Morning Herald*.

> Dear Sir — It is unnecessary to call in the assistance of the police at the ground. The only persons who would benefit by such a step would be the police themselves, who would be handsomely paid for witnessing, from the best point of view, a cricket match which the rest of the public pay for seeing. The company who attend are aristocratic, by wealth or by birth. The police are not required to keep such people in order.

There was another good showdown in the last week of July, when MCC hosted the new Middlesex club for the first time. After the Walker brothers' shunning of Lord's as a home ground, MCC had a point to prove. They instructed their professional bowlers, Grundy and Wootton, to show the visitors no quarter; the pair rolled Middlesex aside for 20 in the first hour, and shared 19 wickets in the game. Middlesex gained their revenge in the return match at Islington, batting all the opening day for 411, and triumphing by an innings.

Elsewhere in Middlesex, cricket-field battles took on a different form. A practice session of the Private Mutual Improvement Society on Uxbridge Common was disrupted by a battalion rally of 250 volunteers of the 24th Middlesex Rifles.

> During the course of drilling, wheeling and advancing in companies, Captain Underwood somehow rode down the wickets. Angry discussion ensured, and the captain's horse was surrounded by an irate group of vexed and accusative cricketers, as well as by a dense crowd of the great unwashed, who were vigorously ungrammatical of their right to be on the Common. On all sides there resounded cries of "Off with him!" and "Tear him off his horse!" Major Hilliard rode up and addressed the throng, assuring them that, if they remained, they would occupy a dangerous situation. — *Uxbridge and West Drayton Gazette*

Three days later, a similar thing happened in Scotland.

> The volunteers having taken up ground near the field of play, at the request of Colonel Tailyour the cricketers drew their stumps and removed to some distance. However, 'the troubles that afflict the just' appeared very applicable, as the skirmishing parties of the battalion

> again interrupted the cricketers who, anxious to avoid the blank cartridge, again drew the stumps. There not being time to seek another field, the game was drawn when it stood thus: Montrose 63 and 104, Brechin 30 and 26 for four. We think it is evident which club would have won had the match been finished. — *Dundee, Perth and Cupar Advertiser*

The main catalyst for cricketing contretemps, though, continued to be the caprice of the match officials. At Chelmsford, one of the home batsmen, on being hit by the ball, found it had lodged in the folds of his jacket. He tried to shake it free, but the Brentwood wicketkeeper pinned his arms down, hoping to complete a catch. There was a scuffle, but the striker managed to grab the ball, and throw it to the ground. He was given out for obstruction; the umpire later told him he should have run six and claimed "lost ball".

At Stonyhurst College, a striker was controversially run out when, having just twisted his ankle and been given a runner, he stood outside his ground. At Stirling, a batsman made room for the wicketkeeper to gather a throw, and was run out for his troubles. Both incidents were considered to be in keeping with the Laws, but contrary to the spirit of cricket.

Nottingham Victoria were one wicket away from beating Beeston Britannia when the Beeston umpire, at the urging of his players, confiscated the ball and declared the match a draw. Two days later, another match in Nottingham was drawn with the last pair at the crease, after the umpire – a local tailor – turned down a convincing appeal in the final over. The local newspaper thundered:

> A Bicester shoemaker, James Tompkins, claimed he was watching a cricket match at between the married and single of Mrs. Froud's Friendly Society, when George Hounslow, another shoemaker, assaulted him. "He asked me a question I did not feel inclined to answer," said Mr. Tompkins. "I made some remark, and he pushed me. He also put his fist in my face, and struck me on the head several times." Mr. Hounslow said he had asked if Mr. Tompkins was hard-up, and wanted a job, and that Mr. Tompkins had replied: "I could employ both Pierson and you too," and pushed *him* over. Mr. Hounslow then received a letter from Mr. Tompkins, promising to take the matter no further if Mr. Hounslow made a public apology in this newspaper. The letter was laid before the bench, and the case was dismissed. — *Bicester Herald*, 15 July

"The game ended in a draw because of the stupidity of the umpire who, being only partly a man, knew more about making breeches than the laws of cricket." A week later, they received a letter arguing that "the laws of cricket are no sealed book to many tailors," and pointing out that Fuller Pilch had been one.

July drew to a close amid wet weather, and the next batch of county matches heavily favoured the bowlers: Mortlock and Willsher claimed seven-wicket hauls, while Griffith, Grundy, James Lillywhite and Tarrant all took ten in a match. The best batting performance came from Kent opener George Kelson, though it did not prevent another defeat.

SURREY v KENT

At The Oval, July 25, 26, 27. **Surrey won by six wickets.** ‡**Kent 104** (W. Mortlock 7-42) **and 169** (G. M. Kelson 83; G. Griffith 6-34); **Surrey 157** (T. Humphrey 44, H. Jupp 32, H. H. Stephenson 48*; E. Willsher 7-47) **and 117-4** (H. Jupp 35). There was a very large number of spectators at the Kennington Oval, including many of the fair sex, for whom we think a tent might be erected for their accommodation, especially when the weather should turn out showery, as was the case on the first day. Mortlock routinely caused trouble with his puzzlers, obtaining seven wickets, even though Surrey fielded rather badly. After Humphrey and Jupp had added 77 for their first wicket, Surrey also batted rather badly, giving up seven wickets to Willsher. In the second innings, the Kent batting for some time prevailed, Mr. Kelson in fine form. There were various changes in bowling, the last being James Street, whose second ball pitched above a foot outside the off stump, and took Mr. Kelson's middle stump. Mr. Kelson returned to the pavilion, where he was presented with two new bats, one from the secretary of each club. Surrey were left 117 to get to win, and were 79 for three at the end of the second day. In less than an hour next morning it was all over.

YORKSHIRE v CAMBRIDGESHIRE

At Sheffield, July 25, 26, 27. **Cambridgeshire won by 55 runs.** ‡**Cambridgeshire 173** (F. C. Pryor 55, T. Hayward 44; I. Hodgson 3-54, L. Greenwood 4-48) **and 119** (G. F. Tarrant 57; L. Greenwood 5-46); **Yorkshire 94** (G. F. Tarrant 6-64, F. R. Reynolds 4-22) **and 143** (J. Berry 39, C. H. Prest 31; G. F. Tarrant 4-56, F. R. Reynolds 4-40). More than ordinary interest was manifested by the lookers on, it being understood that Cambridgeshire intended to win, as they did on the occasion of the first match, at Cambridge. Unfortunately, on the first day, the weather did not hold out. Twice the game was interrupted by heavy rain, and for some time the game was proceeded with under the damping influences of a downfall. Pryor, who had made 64 at Cambridge, again performed his duties skilfully, winning golden opinions from the spectators, and Hayward scored seven off a hit to leg. Roger Iddison, desirous of putting an end to the scoring by the two, bowled his insinuating slows with more than his accustomed smartness, but could not break through. At last, Pryor was out for 55, and the Yorkshire men continued to take wickets, until an increase in the rain caused them to skedaddle. When they returned, the soaked pitch made the ball bounce sluggishly, and Cambridgeshire were all out for 173. Considering the terrific pace of Tarrant and Reynolds, it was a little surprising that Yorkshire held up as long as they did. John Berry was struck a tremendous blow in the ribs by Reynolds, and though he again stood in his crease, it was generally considered that he was not fit to continue. Yorkshire were 74 for four at the close. In the morning, the remainder of the team were vanquished in less than an hour, though they managed to reduce their deficit to below 80, and thus avoided being compelled to bat again. Cambridgeshire scored rather briskly, Tarrant knocking the ball about the green, notwithstanding that the bowling was first-class, and straight on the wicket. Yorkshire were set 199 to win, and reached stumps at 74 for four. The chances of success were thought to be evenly balanced, but the remaining six wickets fell for 20 next day.

KENT v SUSSEX

At Margate, July 28, 29. **Sussex won by nine wickets. ‡Kent 69** (James Lillywhite 6-25) **and 104** (G. Bennett 59; James Lillywhite 5-48, C. H. Ellis 3-12); **Sussex 153** (John Lillywhite 57; E. Willsher 3-30, W. H. Fryer 3-26) **and 21-1.** The new ground at the Clifton Villa Estate had only recently been laid down, and was consequently in anything but first-rate order, but the situation is good, commanding a nice sea view. James Lillywhite caused all manner of difficulty to the Kent batsmen, and John Lillywhite to their bowlers. Sussex established a first-innings majority of 84, and Kent were only able to set them a trifling task to gain victory on the second afternoon. *This was the only season of cricket at the Clifton Villa Estate. The housing of Dalby Square was constructed on the new cricket ground shortly after it was opened.*

John Goodacre, a labourer of Dronfield, was charged by Mr. Samuel Ward with stealing a bat from a cricket field in April 1863. It appeared that the defendant had sold the bat for three shillings, to a youth named Johnson, on Monday 27 June last. Mr. Goodacre claimed to have made the bat himself, and called witnesses to prove his case, but his witnesses only proved to having seen the bat in his possession, and not to having seen him make it. Mr. Ward gave evidence which proved that *he* had made the bat, but he was unable to prove that Mr. Goodacre had stolen it. It was agreed that if the defendant would give up the bat, and reimburse Johnson the money he had got for it, the case would be dismissed. — *Sheffield Independent*, 19 July

Now came the most exciting finish of 1864. Unbeaten Surrey were expected to win, but the pitch which greeted them at Trent Bridge was a far cry from the batsman-friendly surface at The Oval. The contest was reduced to a shootout between two indomitable bowling attacks; only two men reached 30.

NOTTINGHAMSHIRE v SURREY

At Nottingham, July 28, 29. **Surrey won by one wicket. ‡Nottinghamshire 107** (C. Brampton 40; G. Griffith 5-46, T. Sewell 3-22) **and 81** (G. Griffith 6-38, T. Sewell 3-26); **Surrey 127** (T. Sewell 37*; G. Wootton 4-39, J. Grundy 4-42) **and 62-9** (J. Grundy 6-20, J. Jackson 3-17). Having won the first match, at The Oval, so handsomely, Surrey began the match as 6–4 favourites. Nottinghamshire batted first, and though Brampton scored 40 in very good style, no one else reached 20, Griffith's slows earning him five wickets. Surrey, taking their turn, found Wootton and Grundy almost impossible to deal with, but Sewell came in at 73 for eight and scored precious runs, earning a lead of 20. Nottinghamshire then reached 32 for one, but lost five wickets at that score. Griffith took six in the innings, bringing his total to 11 in the match. Surrey were left 62 to win. Grundy disposed of Humphrey by his first ball, but the total had reached 40 for one when an almighty collapse began, eight falling for 18. It was now seven o'clock, the time for drawing the stumps, but shouts of "play it out" came loudly and frequently from the spectators. The umpires decided to continue. Every ball was closely watched, and the excitement was intense. Two byes were scored; one run to tie. Shepherd gained it. Edward Dowson directly after, at half past seven, made the winning hit off Jackson, amid much cheering. It was widely agreed that this match was the sensation of the season.

July had been month of sensations. Not just by Surrey, or W. G. Grace, but by village teams the length and breadth of England, devotedly – even poetically – recorded by local newspapermen. The *North Devon Journal* could turn even the most straightforward match into purple prose:

> "Fine weather, a good wicket and the rigour of the game." So says the captain who, next to his devotions, loves a good game of cricket. North Molton winning the toss, go in. Determined stand by the Brothers Veysey against somewhat erratic bowling. Two o'clock (should have been three, to dodge a shower which resembled crinoline in inflexibility) into town per bus. Lunch, very grateful. Three return to ground; animated appearance thereof. No variegated ladies; one policeman and the parish poultry. Resume the game. Harding and Bankes bat well for Barnstaple,

> the former energetically, the later scientifically. Northerners not so successful in their second innings, a circumstance mainly attributable to improvement in the Barnstaple bowling. Match drawn. North Molton 75 and 35. Barnstaple 49 and 25 without loss.

Reports of close finishes abounded. In Oxford, a thousand turned out to watch the Manchester Unity Order of Odd Fellows chase victory against the Ancient Order of Foresters: with two runs required, the last four wickets fell without addition. Lamberhurst might have clung on for a draw against Hastings, but their last man was discovered to have gone home early, thus also depriving one Mr. Harris of the chance to take all ten wickets. When Alnwick played Tynemouth – a match ignored by the still-sulking Elfin of the *Newcastle Daily Chronicle* – both teams scored 65 and 50.

West Malling staged two absorbing single-wicket games. Mr. Bird, a fruit merchant, scored 17 and 20 against Mr. Terry, a colleague, who made 0 and 0. The agreement was that the loser would buy the winner a slap-up dinner. On account of the early finish, the pair then took on two local butchers. There was time for a full game: the fruiterers made 2 and 2, the butchers 2 and 0, with a Mr. Filmer being run out without facing in both innings.

The *Bury Free Press* was full of admiration for the Hon. Tommy de Gray, who top-scored for Croxton against Norwich without the use of his left arm, which had been crippled by rheumatism. The *South London Chronicle* was similarly impressed by a match between one-armed and one-legged players at Peckham, where over a thousand spectators paid sixpence admission for the benefit of the ground attendant, Ben Neal, who scored 54. The *Maidstone Journal* was less respectful about a women's game at Plaxtol, describing it as "very amusing", and wondering whether talking was allowed on the field. Believe it or not, this was a sign of a modernising attitude: 14 years earlier, the *Dorset County Chronicle* had described a women's match as "a disgusting scene, and altogether discreditable to the district".

AUGUST

The first half of the summer had been a comparatively safe one for cricketers. Dick Daft of Nottinghamshire had taken a knock at Lord's in mid-July, but it was not so severe as to prevent him playing a majestic innings at Crystal Palace a few days later. But a horrific injury at a cricket practice in Nottingham – a batsman named Wilson aimed a vigorous stroke across the line, but succeeded only in striking (and breaking) his own leg – was the beginning of a distinctly painful August. Yorkshire players were among the first to suffer.

SURREY v YORKSHIRE

At The Oval, August 1, 2, 3. **Surrey won by 62 runs. ‡Surrey 145** (J. Caesar 35; R. Iddison 3-13) **and 157** (T. Humphrey 67, W. Mortlock 30; I. Hodgson 3-28, R. Iddison 4-38); **Yorkshire 100** (G. Griffith 3-31, W. Mortlock 3-30, W. Shepherd 3-23) **and 140** (J. Thewlis 51; W. Shepherd 5-43, T. Sewell 3-15). George Anderson had been expected to appear for Yorkshire, but had received a very severe blow between the eyes when playing for Wakefield during the weekend. Surrey, winning the toss, took first innings, and were soon in trouble, especially when Caesar departed for 35. The score had reached 95 for eight when Mr. Burbidge allied with Sewell in a useful stand. The total was raised to 145, which proved an excellent number on a pitch giving no little difficulty. The lightning work of Lockyer accounted for Thewlis, Berry and Iddison, Yorkshire reaching stumps at 86 for eight. The innings closed for 100 exactly, and Surrey immediately built on their lead. Humphrey was badly missed by Berry at slip and, being reprieved, made the Tykes suffer for it. Jupp drove a five off Berry, then hooked one of Atkinson's on to his wicket. Humphrey was stumped for a masterly 67, and was rewarded with a sovereign by the Surrey president. The last five batsmen were out for the addition of 10, leaving Yorkshire to obtain 201 to win. But their run-getting was tardy, and by the end of the second day they were 67 for four. Thewlis went on to make 51, receiving talent money, but William Shepherd's fine bowling ensured that Surrey were the victors.

> Two large haystacks caught fire at Houghton-le-Spring, and owing to a lamentable want of a good supply of water, the flames were allowed to rage at will, the efforts to check the devouring element being utterly unavailing. A cricket match had been about to start in the same field, and it is supposed that one of the smoking fraternity had emptied his pipe near the stacks. The loss is roughly estimated at about £300. — *Newcastle Daily Chronicle*, 9 August

YORKSHIRE v NOTTINGHAMSHIRE

At Bradford, August 4, 5, 6. **Nottinghamshire won by seven wickets. ‡Yorkshire 183** (J. Berry 42, G. Anderson 34; G. Wootton 3-39, R. C. Tinley 5-36) **and 112** (J. Thewlis 44, R. Iddison 31; J. Grundy 3-25); **Nottinghamshire 263** (R. Daft 80, J. Grundy 30, J. Jackson 51, G. Wootton 31; R. Iddison 5-84) **and 33-3.** Both counties brought strong teams to the ground at Horton Road, though Yorkshire were without Greenwood, who was indisposed. Thursday being market day at Bradford, the early attendance was not large. By the efforts of Berry, and later by Anderson, Yorkshire ran up 183, though it would have been rather less had Dick Daft not missed Iddison at square leg, the ball being driven right into his hands. When Nottinghamshire went to the wickets, Daft made a long stand with Grundy, and completely collared the bowling. Jackson also made some splendid play. Atkinson bowled one ball to Daft that was struck back with such force, it hit Atkinson on 'the lower part of the body', and he fell to the ground, unable to move for some minutes. Nottinghamshire established a lead of 80 which, when Yorkshire managed only 112 in their second innings, proved sufficient for victory.

Worse was to come on common land. At Blackheath, a 17-year-old named Godfrey Mills was struck under the right ear and died nine days later. At Farnborough, after the annual game between the bat-makers and ball-makers of The Oval, one Henry Morgan died from an apparent cardiac arrest. A Leicester player with a fondness for beer, Henry Ball, died while fielding at Barwell; the doctors decided his excessive drinking had weakened his heart. A young boy named Spencer had a fit and died after a school match in Warwickshire.

At Fakenham, in Norfolk, the parents of 12-year-old Jonathan Vurley were preparing their supper when their son staggered through the front door. He had been stabbed, he said, on the common: there had been a fight during a game of cricket, and he had hit another boy, Francis Drewell, who had then plunged a pocket-knife into his side. The trial heard that Drewell had started the trouble by refusing to participate in the game if Vurley played, and when

> Anthony Duggan was charged with killing Thomas Howle, after a bet of half a crown on a cricket match at Sheffield. Duggan deposited his money with Howle before the wager, but on winning the bet he discovered that Howle had spent it and gone home in a cab. Duggan challenged him out to fight, and Howle was killed in the ensuing brawl. — *Sheffield Daily Telegraph*, 9 August

the other players sided with Vurley, Drewell had amused himself by hurling handfuls of mud at Vurley's younger brother. Drewell claimed the elder Vurley then rushed upon him, and fell upon the knife, which he was only brandishing in self-defence. All the other boys said the stabbing was intentional. Vurley survived, and Drewell received a two-week sentence for unlawful wounding.

A fight was narrowly averted at Lye in Worcestershire, where the local team played the Beef Eaters – ostensibly a side of gentlemen, though judging from the report in the *Cradley Heath and Stourbridge Observer*, they were anything but.

> The Beef Eaters were evidently strangers to fair play, their behaviour from the commencement being most reprehensible, and their language disgusting, especially towards anyone professing a knowledge of the noble and manly game of cricket. The Institute were 17 from victory when the Beef Eaters created a dispute. Though every point was conceded to them, they persisted in not playing the game out, some of them proposing that it should be settled by a pugilistic encounter. The Institute not complying, the Beef Eaters walked off without delivering a ball, or the price of one.

In Derbyshire, Chesterfield found themselves on the wrong end of a huge Clay Cross total, and went home early, according to the *Derbyshire Courier*, "with their tempers a little ruffled, not being able to reconcile themselves to the idea of joining the Clay Cross players at supper". There was also discord in Leicestershire, where Uppingham Rovers failed to turn up for their game with Garendon, and in Oxfordshire, where a team of university servants were denied victory when the scorers misread a tally of two no-balls as 11. At least bloodshed was averted.

Morbid fascination notwithstanding, August's chief cricketing spectacle was that traditional English favourite, the exhibition match. In high summer, the higher social classes left London for spa towns or seaside resorts. Canterbury fitted neither category, but its size, history and proximity to London still made it a fashionable destination, and St Lawrence, east of the city centre, had become MCC's de facto outground. Lord's hosted two dozen high-profile games in the first half of 1864 – but none after Grace's success for South Wales against I Zingari at the end of July. In August, Canterbury was the centre of events.

Canterbury Week had its roots in an 1841 fixture, at the Beverly Ground, between a Kent side starring Fuller Pilch and an England XI selected by MCC. The contest proved so popular that three first-class games were staged the following year: Kent v England, Kent v Sussex, and Gentlemen of Kent v Gentlemen of England. In 1847, the venue was switched to St Lawrence, and though the Sussex fixture was soon dropped, Canterbury Week was firmly established as the nation's foremost cricket festival: a Monday-to-Friday exhibition of the very best of the sport.

The 1864 matches fell some way short of that mark – at least as far as the struggling Kent side were concerned. The England XI smashed them by an innings and 83 runs, with Wootton taking 13 for 48. This was hard on the organisers, who had told the public to expect a "powerful" home team, and had tried to ensure an even contest by allowing Kent two extra players. The second day was beset by a ferocious storm which tore down several marquees, and torrential rain prevented any post-match promenading. Further humiliation came in the gentlemen's game, with Lt. Henry Arkwright – the MCC bowler shortly to meet an unfortunate end on Mount Blanc – claiming nine wickets in the first innings and five in the second, as Kent went down by 241 runs.

Canterbury Week was not Kent's only cricketing attraction of high summer. In Stockbury, a crowd turned up to see two members of the local club take on two complete beginners. The novices managed just nine runs, but to everyone's delight, they won by an innings, bowling the cricketers out for 1, 0, 0 and 0.

Having trounced Kent at St Lawrence, seven of the England XI raced to Manchester to take part in the second of 1864's games between the professionals of the North and South.

George Mitchell, a fishmonger of Bishop's Stortford, was charged with stealing a cricket ball, belonging to a lad named Frank Judd, at Rickling Green. Mr. Judd and several others were playing at cricket, and when the ball passed the net, Mitchell picked it up, put it in his cart, and drove off. When the boys asked for it, he denied all knowledge, but a policeman was summoned, searched the cart, and found the ball lying between two hampers. The Bench sentenced Mitchell to a month's hard labour. —*Essex Standard*, 10 August

At Manchester, August 11, 12, 13. **North won by nine wickets. ‡South 158** (E. W. Pooley 30*; R. C. Tinley 5-52, J. Jackson 3-23) **and 154** (H. H. Stephenson 36, G. Griffith 36; G. F. Tarrant 4-55, R. C. Tinley 4-92); **North 296** (T. Hayward 66, R. P. Carpenter 52) **and 17-1.**

The Northerners established their superiority in an innings lasting 221 overs, with Carpenter, Hayward and Tarrant – Cambridgeshire was, at that time, considered part of the North – the highest scorers. At the end of the game, half the players travelled to London for a pair of matches at The Oval.

Surrey beat an England XI by nine wickets – perhaps not the achievement it sounds, given that all but two of the Surrey team had represented England. Teddy Grace got the invitation side going with a gorgeous innings that only ended when Lockyer relinquished the gloves and bowled, but Humphrey and Jupp eclipsed Grace with an opening stand of 129 that put Surrey in a winning position. They benefited from the woeful fielding of Brampton, who dropped a sitter, then prevented Dick Daft from catching one by running into him.

Rain spoiled the game between Surrey and the South, played for the benefit of Daniel Day, keeper of the Antelope Inn (and ground) at Southampton; all the professionals donated their fees to him. Mortlock made a century for Surrey, and his team-mate Frederick Miller took a few wickets with his underarm slows before a testimonial dinner in his own honour, at which he was presented with a silver vase worth fifty guineas. Day's profit was more than £200.

The Oval's best attendance of August, though, came when it hosted a match between one-armed and one-legged players. Since the Peckham game the previous month, there had been a spate of these fixtures. On 11 August, at Tunbridge Wells, all the participants were pensioners. A fortnight later, the *General Intelligencer* found humour in a match at Southsea:

> One of the players unfortunately fell and broke his leg. The unfeeling spectators burst out in roars of laughter. The man was carried off the field, and it was necessary to amputate the leg. Fortunately, it was made of wood.

Such insensitivity was mild compared with the report published by the *Evening Standard* after the Oval game, which took place at the end of the month.

More than 3,000 showed up for the Kennington fixture, not with the aim of watching cricket, but to enjoy a *danse macabre.*

> The mirth created by the batsmen making their runs, and the more ludicrous attempts to field the ball, was general. The casualties of tumbling down and cannoning against each other caused much amusement, though each instance, we are glad to say, proved harmless. Nevertheless there were several good hits, which elicited loud shouts of applause. Imagine a one-leg man attempting to run after a ball: he breaks his wooden leg and the whole of the spectators are convulsed with laughter, which is increased when one of his opponents picks him up and carries him on his back to the retiring-room.

Elsewhere, exhibition games were taken more seriously. At Torquay, a concerted effort was made to launch a cricket festival to rival Canterbury Week. Devon was much further from London than Kent, but the seafront at Torquay had been connected to the railway network in 1859, and the English Riviera arguably had a good deal more going for it than spa-less, sea-less Canterbury.

The idea had been born in April, during the annual meeting of Torquay Cricket Club. They had previously experimented with a Ladies' Day, but it had incurred a loss, and they decided to amalgamate it into a fully-fledged Torquay Week, immediately before the annual regatta in August. Six days of cricket were scheduled, the second to be a Ladies' Day. "This is the first attempt in the West to attempt anything of the kind," wrote the *Western Times*. "Tuesday afternoon will be devoted to the ladies who, though nothing with the bat, will have a great catch in opening the new ballroom."

Torquay began the week with an innings win over the Plymouth Garrison, followed by the ball, in the club's brand new pavilion. The occasion delighted the *Western Times*: "Flowers of all hues and forms were entwined with ivy and other evergreens, in wreaths and festoons that encircled walls and windows,

> Ellen Hurst, a masculine-looking woman of no fixed address, was charged with stealing a pair of cricketing trousers, the property of the Wolverhampton Cricket Club professional. The prisoner had stopped for some ale at a public house, but had left with a leathern bag containing the trousers, four shillings, and two spoons. — *Birmingham Daily Gazette*, 12 August

and stretched across the room from side to side." The *Torquay Directory* correspondent was rather less complimentary.

> The band of the Garrison seized upon their instruments. Their skill, it must be admitted, cannot be compared to that of Orpheus. When he tuned his lyre, it is said that even the most rapid rivers ceased to flow, the savage beasts of the forest forgot their wildness and the mountains moved to listen. But when the officers played their pipes, only execrable and diabolical sounds were the results. People were greatly astonished, as well they might have been, at the incongruous medley of tones that were produced. It was enough to turn any number of Babbages – the genius inventor of the famous calculating machine – into fit subjects for the mental institution at Colney Hatch.

A two-day victory by the Gentlemen of Devon against the Gentlemen of Dorset was to have been followed by a theatre performance by members of the West of England Histrionic Club. But a sudden illness swept through the company and, at the very last minute, the Torquay cricketers were pressed into taking the stage to attempt The Odyssey. The *Torquay Directory* described their efforts as "a screaming farce". Relieved of their dramatic duties, Torquay closed the festival with a game against a team from Cornwall. Though Boconnoc were thrashed, they could not possibly have been a worse side than the Gentlemen of Cornwall who, at Plymouth the following week, lost to their Devonian counterparts by an innings and 196 runs, having fielded only seven players.

Cornwall were not the only lesser county to have a tricky time of things. Carmarthenshire went one worse by bringing only six players to a fixture with Pembrokeshire at Tenby. Ceredigion dismissed Montgomeryshire for 40 and 64, but still lost by one run. Buckinghamshire were well pleased with their first day at Islington, racking up 294 and dismissing Middlesex for 76, helped by a hundred from Edward Austen-Leigh (a great-nephew of Jane Austen), a half-century from Charles Marsham (the proposer of the overarm vote) and five wickets from MCC professional Tom Hearne. Middlesex followed on, but after John Dyne departed for eight, everyone else reached double figures in a total of 463. Buckinghamshire got nowhere near their target of 246, and the few punters who had backed the home team at 20 to one enjoyed a bonanza.

Middlesex's next game was at Hove, against a Sussex side in top form. Sussex had just swept aside Hampshire – and James Lillywhite had played the game of his life. When he walked out to open the batting, his first-class average for Sussex was 8.19. Only on three occasions had he scored as many as 20.

SUSSEX v HAMPSHIRE

At Hove, August 11, 12, 13. **Sussex won by ten wickets. ‡Sussex 280** (James Lillywhite 105, H. M. Hyndman 58, John Lillywhite 45; E. L. Ede 4-79, W. Humphrey 3-61) **and 33-0; Hampshire 164** (G. M. Ede 52; James Lillywhite 5-63, C. H. Ellis 5-71) **and 148** (H. Holmes 71; James Lillywhite 4-50, C. H. Ellis 3-74). This match was utterly dominated by Mr. Jem Lillywhite, who followed an innings of 105 with nine Hampshire wickets. The loudest applause came when he reached 51, and an announcement was made that he had reached a half-century for the first time. This seemed rather to unsettle his nerves, and for a time he played decidedly fluky, giving a fair chance to Mr. Maturin. It was some time until that fielder gained satisfaction: he took the ball when Mr. Lillywhite was 105, and bowled him. Two sovereigns were collected for the innings, one from Mr. John Lillywhite. On the second day, Hampshire proceeded to 152 for six, whereupon Mr. Lillywhite made another telling contribution, taking four wickets in ten minutes. Hampshire followed their innings, and Mr. Smith was run out the very first ball. The next three were sent back by Mr. Lillywhite, who also caught out Mr. Maturin. And after Mr. Lillywhite, for the second time in the match, bowled Edward Bowen, who thus completed his spectacles, the Sussex men made short work of the task of making 33 to win.

SUSSEX v MIDDLESEX

At Hove, August 15, 16, 17. **Sussex won by three wickets. ‡Middlesex 244** (T. Case 34, T. Hearne 56, W. H. Benthall 46, I. D. Walker 31*; James Lillywhite 4-96, R. Fillery 5-40) **and 118** (James Lillywhite 5-45, C. H. Ellis 5-67); **Sussex 194** (G. Wells 82, C. Payne 31; R. D. Walker 5-54) **and 170-7** (H. M. Hyndman 62, C. H. Ellis 33*; R. D. Walker 6-76). Middlesex scored very fast, in spite of capital bowling and equally excellent fielding. Hearne was the largest contributor to their 244, but most of the other batsmen succeeded in putting on double figures. By seven o'clock, Sussex were 55 for two, and in the morning Wells made his score up to 82 by a splendid display, and Payne played a very pretty innings of 31. Though Middlesex took a lead of 50, in the second innings they were not fortunate, having to contend with bowling and fielding almost perfect. Thus Sussex were left 169 to win – a very even game, promising an exciting finish. They had lost one wicket by the end of the second day's play, and on the third, Henry Hyndman proved to be the key to the result. When he had obtained one run only, he was dropped by Henry Wheeler, and very courteously took his hat off to him, thanking him very much. Mr. Smith was caught off the bat in front of the wicket by Pooley, the wicketkeeper, one of the most amusing pieces of fiddling we have seen for many a day. Mr. Hyndman made several immense hits to leg, and had about five lives before departing for 62. Ellis and Payne kept the ball moving till they had reduced the required runs to six, whereupon Ellis hit one of Hearne's to the corner, a splendid drive, and they ran all six amidst immense cheering.

The good mood at Hove did not last long. The day after the match, the Gentlemen of Sussex – captained by the county secretary, Bridger Stent – hosted the Quidnuncs. Hyndman failed with the bat, then toiled in the field as Henry Biron, who had recently ended his Kent career with a solitary fifty to his name, plundered 214. Stent then did the accounts for August's two county games, and found each had incurred expenses of around £100. The club had only 100 shillings in the bank. In a last-ditch attempt to stave off bankruptcy, Stent appealed in the newspapers for donations from "all who admire manly exercise", while his team decamped to the Antelope at Southampton.

HAMPSHIRE v MIDDLESEX

At Southampton, August 29, 30. **Middlesex won by ten wickets. ‡Middlesex 296** (T. Case 45, R. A. Bayford 92, R. D. Walker 52, Extras 48; J. S. Frederick 4-45) **and 1-0; Hampshire 163** (J. S. Frederick 37; T. Hearne 4-71, R. D. Walker 3-48) **and 133** (J. S. Frederick 44; W. Catling 4-33). Middlesex went in first, Thomas Case punishing Teddy Ede's slows rather smartly, and Robert Bayford displaying some powerful hitting and obdurate defence in making his highest score. Hampshire felt the absence of their usual long-stop, as the byes which were lost constituted an innings of themselves. The actual time devoted to play on the first day was little more than four hours. Steps must be taken to remedy this squandering of valuable time, which breaks faith with the public.

We have received the following — "Please publish the challenge of four men, whose united ages are 324, to play a game of cricket. The men played on Meopham Green in 1805, and are open to play against any four men, from any parish in Kent, on Meopham Green, for love or money. The players are J. Cooper, Wm. Johnson, Thos. Trudder and Wm. Benstead. Please write to Thomas Hills, Meopham Green." — *Maidstone Journal*, 29 August

When Hampshire batted the next day, Hearne was on the spot, taking four wickets. Mr. Ede made an ugly hit to leg, and started, calling Mr. Frederick, but like the spirits from the vast deep, he would not come. Mr. Ede slipped and could not get back, and Pooley put down his wicket. Mr. Frederick hit a sixer clean out of the ground, against the houses, which elicited a cheer, but the home side had to follow their innings. Again Mr. Frederick batted splendidly, and there was a rare laugh at Pooley's expense when he put off the bails and ran away with the ball, only for the umpire to give the batsman "in". The Hampshire innings concluded with the scores level, and Middlesex's winning run came by the bowling of a wide.

Middlesex were not the only team to reach a one-run target courtesy of a wide: that same afternoon, the How-d'ye-do's beat Bromsgrove Grammar School in identical fashion. Hampshire thus completed a winless season, unless one counted a visit to The Oval in May when, with the assistance of three extra men, they defeated Surrey. Since Surrey were widely held to be the strongest of all the county teams, it seems likely the Hampshire players *did* count it.

SEPTEMBER

Though the Victorian autumn was far from balmy, September 1864 still saw big matches and big crowds. After a draw at Sleaford in June, and a heavy defeat at Old Trafford in August, the men of the South were anxious to restore their reputation in the third game, at Islington. But several key players of the North – including the entire Cambridgeshire contingent – said they did not want to travel, and the outcome was a mismatch. James Lillywhite continued his fine form of the previous month, the Northern batsmen finding no answer to his left-arm slows. There would have been two full innings on the first day, but for a last-wicket stand of 49 between Bennett and Sewell, which took the South's innings into the next morning. Jonathan Joy was the only Northerner to get to grips with the bowling, top-scoring twice in an innings defeat. For the Southerners, honour was satisfied.

At Islington, September 5, 6. **South won by an innings and 29 runs**. ‡**North 63** (James Lillywhite 5-24, T. Sewell 5-36) **and 83** (J. Joy 30; James Lillywhite 3-38, T. Sewell 3-21, T. Hearne 3-12); **South 175** (G. Bennett 73; G. Wootton 5-69, J. Grundy 3-27).

A week later, there was an end-of-term atmosphere as many of the big names mustered at Godalming to play a benefit match for Julius Caesar, an enormously popular cricketer among professionals and public alike. The match was a damp draw, but during a banquet in Caesar's honour, Murray Marshall – a local dignitary – presented him with a gold watch and a purse of sovereigns.

> Mr. Samuel Watts brought a case against Mr. Frederick Hill, the proprietor of the Surrey club-house at The Oval. Mr. Watts said he had accompanied a group of children to a match at the ground, and on their departure, Mr. Hill's dog had seized him by the trousers behind, and not only bit through them, but also his flesh. Mr. Hill replied that there had been 40,000 visitors to The Oval that week, and the only one to have been bitten was Mr. Watts. The Chairman suggested Mr. Hill make Mr. Watts some compensation. Mr. Hill offered a half-sovereign, and the complainant expressed himself well satisfied. — *Morning Advertiser*, 15 September

Happy though Caesar's benefit was, it caused consternation in Oxfordshire, where Wallingford were playing a team from the Master Butchers' Club for a substantial wager. The Butchers had signed up Surrey openers Humphrey and Jupp, so they magnanimously agreed that Wallingford could field 22 men. But on the morning of the game, it transpired that Humphrey and Jupp had decided to play at Godalming instead – and the hapless butchers were minced. Only one of their number came out of the game with any credit: the prolific Charles Absolon, who blagged a game and bagged 14 wickets.

The Graces were conspicuously absent from these fixtures. After the South Wales tour, neither Henry nor Gilbert ventured outside the Bristol area. They had all the cricket they wanted among their local clubs – and, in any case, were not prominent enough to merit a fee for a guest appearance. The opposite was true of Teddy, who had played in both Canterbury Week matches, then starred for the England XI against Surrey. He managed to squeeze in one club game, for Lansdown, carrying his bat for 82, then taking 13 wickets in an innings victory – but for the most part, he was available to the highest bidder.

In the second week of September, the secretary of Carmarthenshire reached deep into his pockets to secure Teddy's services for a needle match with Glamorganshire at Neath. The standard was far beneath Teddy and, according to the *Carmarthen Journal*, he barely broke sweat in earning his team a winning position.

> Mr Grace drove the ball all over the field, a large concourse of spectators gazing in wonder at his sensational hitting. In the first innings, he was cut short for 34, and in the second, he had made 41 in his usual free

George Bax, while labouring at the East Cliff in Ramsgate, was nearly hit by a cricket ball, belonging to Joseph Hubbard, who was playing a game on the adjacent green. Bax, somewhat put out, picked the ball up and threw it into the sea. Mr. Hubbard and his friends spent half an hour splashing about, trying to retrieve it, but in vain, so laid a charge against Bax for malicious destruction of property worth 7s 6d. But Bax's workmates testified that Mr. Hubbard had been repeatedly cautioned not to play at the site, and the bench dismissed the charge. — *Thanet Advertiser*, 17 September

> style, when he apparently deliberately ran himself out. Mr. Grace also fielded and bowled brilliantly, taking six wickets and three catches in Glamorganshire's first innings. They only appeared to any advantage in the latter stages of the game, no doubt in consequence of the early departure of Mr. Grace.

Teddy's decision to go home early allowed a relieved Glamorganshire – nine down, and still 65 short of victory – to hang on for a draw. Gilbert, meanwhile, had helped himself to 27 wickets in a single match, bowling unchanged for Clifton against a Bristol Grammar School XXII. But if any game illustrated the astounding competitiveness of the Graces, it was played at Hanham, against Bitton, on Saturday 17 September 1864.

The brothers had often turned out for Hanham, and this time three had been invited to play: Henry (31), Alfred (24) and Gilbert (16). Gilbert's autobiography recalls only himself and Henry, which seems a trifle harsh on Alfred, a markedly inferior player. As they were about to depart in their pony-trap, Teddy appeared in his cricket gear. "It's no good," said Henry. "The other side won't stand another one of us." But Teddy came anyway – and got a game with Bitton.

What a game it was. Bitton's first-innings total of 81 put them in charge, and they were eventually set a target of ten. Teddy told Henry he would hit the winning runs from the first over, perhaps even the first ball. But Henry sent down a shooter, Teddy was bowled, and Bitton fell to 0 for 4. Three runs came, then three byes – and the remaining six wickets fell without addition. *Sporting Life* called it "one of the best examples of the uncertainty of the noble game".

> We sometimes describe boating in the summer, and skating in the winter, on the river, but on Monday a hitherto undescribed scene was witnessed: some boys playing cricket on the bed of the river, opposite the inn. But even as this beautiful scene was unfolding, the pavilion at Uppingham was broken into and a quantity of cricket balls, a belt and some shoe horns were stolen. Sgt. Briggs apprehended a tramp named John Wilmott the following day. He was remanded till the petty sessions at Empingham. Seven balls and the belt have been recovered. —*Stamford Mercury*, 16 September

HANHAM

1st innings		2nd innings	
W. G. Grace c Grace b Fraser	3	b Grace	10
Howard run out	6	run out	1
Wright not out	16	c Fraser b Grace	0
Fry b Fraser	0	run out	1
Richmond c Jones b Grace	1	st Pillinger b Grace	0
A. Grace c and b Fraser	2	b Pillinger	5
H. Grace b Fraser	7	b Grace	3
Bucknall run out	1	b Pillinger	3
Morris b Grace	0	st Pillinger b Grace	8
Bryant run out	2	not out	1
Sealey b Grace	10	lbw b Grace	1
Extras	3	Extras	6
Total	**51**	Total	**39**

BITTON

1st innings		2nd innings	
E. M. Grace b H. Grace	7	b H. Grace	0
Lillington run out	2	b W. G. Grace	0
Pillinger b H. Grace	10	b H. Grace	0
Jones b Howard	33	b W. G. Grace	0
Fraser b W. G. Grace	2	run out	0
Bush b H. Grace	3	run out	3
Weston b H. Grace	3	c and b W. G. Grace	0
Somerville run out	7	b W. G. Grace	0
Godfrey not out	3	b W. G. Grace	0
Bush b W. G. Grace	0	not out	0
Cox b W. G. Grace	2	b W. G. Grace	0
Extras	9	Extras	3
Total	**81**	Total	**6**

There was one fixture remaining in the brothers' season: a visit by West Gloucestershire to Cheltenham College. Every College wicket fell to a Grace, and Teddy smashed a carefree 139 ("for which I presented myself with a new bat"). Gilbert made 29, and no one else reached double-figures. Gilbert's season statistics make for extraordinary reading.

W. G. GRACE IN 1864

33 matches · 1,306 runs · average 29.68 · 2 hundreds · 5 fifties
189 wickets · 21 five-wicket hauls · 37 catches · 2 stumpings

It is perhaps surprising to the modern reader to find schools playing cricket after the summer holidays. But school football was in its infancy – 1864 was the first year football had an agreed code of laws – and only the most prestigious schools played rugby. For most, September was a cricketing month. A bizarre match took place in Lancashire: Whalley Grammar School were dismissed for 13 by Blackburn, but kept the first-innings lead to just three; they then racked up 124, and bowled Blackburn out a second time, for seven. The children of Mr. Mate's School in Kent returned to action with a match between day pupils and boarders, a day boy named Thorpe scoring 51 and taking 15 wickets.

Many clubs wrapped up their seasons as they had begun them, by organising scratch games amongst themselves. The local papers had no less an appetite for cricketing news, and hungrily reported on such fixtures as married v single, sons v fathers, over 5ft 8in v under 5ft 8in, Whigs v Tories, singers v instrumentalists, toolmakers v sheepshearers, and even bearded v barefaced.

Even so, there was still some good cricket, especially when the United England team were playing. Against Hastings, George Griffith thumped all four balls of an over onto the roofs of houses opposite the ground, running six each time. Against Margate, Mortlock returned match figures of 53.3–11–53–17. But when the United men travelled to Newcastle to toy with a Northumberland XXII, they received an almighty shock. The hosts' innings contained seven ducks, ten single-figure scores, four between 10 and 15 – and an unbeaten 120 from a young man named John Grey. The professionals lost by 15 wickets, and unanimously agreed that Grey's innings was the finest they had witnessed all season. It must have distracted them from the freezing wind – for England was now beset by autumn gales. When the United England bandwagon rolled on to Bradford, the *Bradford Observer* correspondent could barely stand.

> We should not have so many matches played in September. In the summer, the game may be interrupted for a while by overcrowding, but in September the batsmen may hit where they like without the slightest fear of the ball ever coming in contact with anything like the ghost of a spectator. Would it not be an improvement, next year, to provide the players with a much larger luncheon before the game, thus dissuading them from going near the field at all? Even the most enthusiastic of

> cricket supporters would prefer remaining quietly at home to exposing themselves to attacks of bronchitis, diphtheria and rheumatism by standing in a field watching a match at this time of year.

But there was certainly heat at Redhill, where bets had been laid, when the last pair of batsmen plucked out the stumps on the stroke of six o'clock, saying their dinner had been ordered at six and they didn't want to risk incurring the wrath of the cook. Some matches did not even reach that hour. At Hawkshead in Westmorland, Broughton were 11 for 4, chasing 137, when a decision displeased them, and they quit the game altogether. In Lancashire, Tongue went home when a call went against them at Firwood, while Ormskirk refused to continue their game with Southport until an umpire was replaced.

The cricketers of Chipping Norton, in Oxfordshire, were overjoyed to discover that H. H. Stephenson, the Surrey and England all-rounder, had moved to the village – and wasted no time in recruiting him for their late-season grudge match against Witney. Hundreds turned up to see him in action, but the Witney umpire had other ideas, giving Stephenson out lbw to a ball that hit him in the chest. The *Bicester Observer* wrote that "a more unsatisfactory decision has never before come under our notice". But such griping paled into insignificance compared with a brouhaha that was brewing in Scotland.

Lord Kinnaird of Rossie Priory was a well-known landowner, and a cricket fan. He was something of a philanthropist, throwing fetes for the poor families of Dundee and Perth, and founding Rossie Cricket Club, which regularly held matches on his estate. In September 1864, Kinnaird met Queen Victoria when she unveiled a statue in Perth, the chimney sweeps of Dundee were invited to the Priory for a garden party, and the Rossie team were looking forward to hosting a match against Inchmartine.

> The plaintiff, Mr. Restall, was playing cricket with his friends in Farnham Park when the defendant, Mr. Halfacre, came and took away the stumps, and refused to give them up, stating that the Bishop of Winchester had instructed him to take them. There being no evidence that the Bishop had made any such order, His Honour ordered the stumps to be returned, or 2s 6d to be paid to the plaintiff. — *Surrey Advertiser*, 24 September

Then came a letter. Kinnaird wrote to the Rossie secretary, expressly forbidding his team to play Inchmartine, owing to the "too free use of spirituous liquors" by that club. His Lordship, a keen supporter of the temperance movement, had heard that whiskey was provided at Inchmartine games, and feared that they would bring it to *his* game, and might tempt the Rossie men to take up the habit. He had already forbidden one of his estate workers from joining Inchmartine, and his latest edict drew ire from every quarter. The *Perthshire Constitutional* was typical, though by no means alone.

> Nothing comes more naturally to some persons than to make themselves ridiculous. Lord Kinnaird has not only made a fool of himself, but has tried to traduce the character of men superior to himself in all respects, save social position, and has cast a slur on the highly respected name of Mrs. Fergusson Blair, who provides the food and drink at the Inchmartine ground. It was quite open to His Lordship to exercise the petty tyranny for which he is famous, and refuse the use of his ground, but to give such a contemptible reason was surely travelling out of his way. We hardly understand the bitter hostility with which His Lordship regards the hospitality of the Inchmartine club, unless he takes it as an affront to his own Rossie Priory, which is famous for its stinginess.

The Inchmartine secretary, David Morrison, called a meeting. There was a massive turnout, not least because all the newspapers in Scotland sent a reporter. First, Morrison read a letter he had sent to Lord Kinnaird on behalf of the club, to the effect that unless an apology was forthcoming, His Lordship was not permitted at the Inchmartine cricket field, nor at their curling pond – one of his favourite haunts. Then came the turn of the chairman, Mr. Anderson.

> "I defy the noble Lord to bring forward a single instance of intoxication. An insult has been cast upon us, and our fair fame is destroyed in the eyes of the world. At Inchmartine, as at Rossie, the brewer's cart is not allowed on the ground for the sale of liquor. All eatables and drinkables are kindly and most cordially supplied by Mrs. Blair. Everywhere we play, we receive the same kind hospitality – except at Rossie, where the cricket ground is kept largely pure and free from contamination by meat and drink, chimney sweeps evidently being well pleased merely with tea and cookies. Is the explanation to be found in jealousy? Does Lord Kinnaird, with all his show of philanthropy, feel eclipsed by the popularity of Mrs. Blair?"

To widespread astonishment, Mrs. Blair herself then walked calmly into the meeting, informed the chairman that she had brought only "the breastplate of truth", and took the floor.

> "Gentlemen, it is unusual for a female to take part in meetings of this nature, but I wish to express my opinion of Lord Kinnaird's most unwarrantable attack. Time was when he would not have dared to breathe my name but in deepest respect. Had he acted like a Christian, and as a gentleman, he would have written to me in a friendly manner. But he has chosen to take umbrage. This clearly shows his animus."

The effect of Mrs. Blair's speech was electric. Here was a respectable woman, complaining that a noble Lord had slandered her in public. Every paper in England carried the story, from the *Monmouthshire Merlin* to the *Shipping and Mercantile Gazette*, and the coverage in the Scottish press filled more column inches than any other event of the year. The *Dundee Courier* felt Mrs. Blair's accusation – that Kinnaird had deliberately sought to injure an unprotected lady – was far worse than His Lordship's charge of whiskey-drinking. The *Montrose Standard* lambasted the Rossie cricketers: "whose principles are so apt to be weakened by the sight of whiskey that Lord Kinnaird must watch over them with ever-wakeful earnestness". It added, for good measure, that Mrs. Blair had given Lord Kinnaird "a moral horse-whipping". All the papers reported Mr. Anderson's comments about chimney sweeps "being well pleased merely with tea and cookies".

The chimney sweeps did not like that one bit, and called their own meeting, to condemn the insult. Mr. Anderson and Mrs. Blair were tipped off, and sent letters of apology to be read. The sweeps forgave Mrs. Blair – they could hardly

> Arthur Kite, of Twickenham, was summoned to the Bench for using abusive language to Mr. Thomas Cogsmight, a resident of Twickenham Green. Mr. Cogsmight testified that one of his windows had been broken by a cricket ball. Kite came to fetch the ball, but Mr. Cogsmight angrily said he intended to keep it, to which Kite replied "Who the — are you?" The Chairman ruled that Mr. Cogsmight had no right to detain the ball. The case was dismissed. — *West Middlesex Herald*, 24 September

do otherwise, since to reject the apology of a woman was injurious in itself – but not Mr. Anderson. They thought his letter a sham: "He may send a letter like that to the farmers of the Carse of Gowrie, but not the sweeps of Dundee."

Now it was the farmers' turn to take offence. For some time afterwards, they took to shouting "There goes Lord Kinnaird's bodyguard!" whenever a chimney sweep passed by.

Kinnaird had his supporters. A medical officer, writing in the *Perthshire Advertiser*, said it was right for the "upper and educated classes to set a good example to the lower and less favoured".

There remained the question of what the outcome should be. *The Scotsman* said it was a matter of gallantry that the lady should have the last word. The *Falkirk Herald* did not expect Kinnaird to apologise, "as we presume he is imbued with Baronial stubbornness". His Lordship's response – he invited Arbroath Cricket Club to come and play Rossie, and got them drunk on pale ale – surprised everyone except the chimney sweeps, who claimed it was well known that Lord Kinnaird drank, and that they were always trying to persuade him to stop.

While all this was going on, the only first-class county match of September slipped quietly by at Middlesbrough. It was not a match of note, by any means: though Yorkshire had been below their best all season, Kent maintained their perfect losing record.

YORKSHIRE v KENT

At Middlesbrough, September 19, 20, 21. **Yorkshire won by four wickets. ‡Kent 195** (W. Goodhew 52, G. C. Dickins 34*, J. S. Payne 32; R. Iddison 4-72) **and 110** (R. Iddison 4-32); **Yorkshire 212** (J. Joy 74; W. McCanlis 4-67) **and 95-6** (J. Berry 41*; E. Willsher 4-22). "The best-laid schemes of mice and men aft gang aglee", and the eleven Yorkshiremen who assembled on the ground were not the team announced on the bills for this match – an extra one so far as the annual contests between the counties are concerned. Kent went first to the wickets, and Mr. Fryer was very easily run out, the fault all his own. Mr. Kelson cut one of Iddison's full on to his own ear, with an audible "crump" on the cartilage. Goodhew played beautifully for 52, before a last-wicket stand of 66 raised the total to 195. Yorkshire replied with 212, for which they had to thank Joy, who hit 74, the only half-century of his life. Atkinson and Iddison then brought calamity upon the Kentish men, sharing seven wickets, and restricting them to 110. Yorkshire were left the not at all formidable number of 94 to get. This they were not long in accomplishing, Berry making, in a brilliant fashion, no less than 41 not out.

At least the Kent players would have dined well on their way home. Spiers and Pond, the sponsors of England's first tour to Australia, had arrived in London to develop their business interests. They rented an office at Charing Cross station – which had opened in January – and announced they would be running a refreshment stand at every station on the London, Chatham and Dover Railway. They also said they were hoping to arrange another big-name tour of Australia, for the Baptist preacher Charles Spurgeon – or, should he decline, for Tom Sayers, a bare-knuckle boxer. In the event, they got neither. Spurgeon was in the midst of a rift with the Church of England; Sayers had contracted tuberculosis, and died the following year.

The autumn was equally tough for George Marshall, who had assumed the Spiers and Pond role as organiser of Parr's tour to Australia. He was to some extent the architect of his own downfall: Billy Caffyn had proven so popular on the tour that he stayed with Melbourne CC as a coach, with the club guaranteeing his prosperity by setting him up in the cricketing goods trade. Caffyn's business was so successful, it put Marshall's in the shade, and at the end of September, Marshall was declared bankrupt.

Caffyn struggled to adjust to life in Melbourne. After a year, he moved to Sydney, where he coached, played, and ran a hairdressing business. His fiancée came out to join him, but struggled with the heat, and two of their four children died. They returned to England in 1871, and Caffyn regretted staying away so long. "I made a mistake," he wrote. "I have nothing to thank Australia for."

Another key figure on England's tour, Tom Wills – who bolstered several of the weaker Australian oppositions, then captained Canterbury and

> The defendants played a cricket match at Petworth, and on their journey home, at 11 o'clock at night, they commenced holloaing, singing etc. A constable told them to cease, and was struck in the chest, but evidence showed that he had commenced the attack. — *West Sussex Gazette*, 29 September

Otago – suffered even greater ignominy. After Parr's men set sail, Wills travelled home to Queensland, where he was abandoned by his fiancée (for being a womaniser) and his company trustees (for being a dreadful manager). Though he was a pioneering figure in Aboriginal and women's cricket, he was dogged by allegations of promiscuity, cheating, drunkenness and an illegal bowling action. In 1880, he stabbed himself to death with a pair of scissors.

As September drew to a close, and another Little Ice Age winter began to touch the British landscape with its frigid fingers, there was a first-class fixture still to be played: a fourth North v South match, at Newmarket. The sports reporters of the northern counties, though, now had their minds elsewhere. The *Leeds Mercury* devoted considerable space to a knur and spell contest on the Kirkstall Road, which was witnessed by 1,000 spectators. The North, it seemed, had given up on cricket for the year.

OCTOBER

The South, meanwhile, had given up on knur and spell. At least, that was the impression given by John Wisden, who had decided to remove the pastime – as well as all other non-cricketing content – from the second edition of his *Almanack*, which he spent most of October compiling. The first advertisement appeared on 1 October, in the *Wells Journal*.

> CRICKETING OUTFITTERS. JOHN WISDEN & Co., 2 New Coventry-st., London, W. have a large selection of Cricketing materials, Footballs, Croquet, Skittles, Rackets, Quoits, Boxing-gloves, Dumb Bells, Clubs, &c. THE CRICKETER'S ALMANACK for 1865. Price 1s., post-free 1s. 1d. Illustrated price list free.

Wisden intended to publish the 1865 *Almanack* on New Year's Day and, by November, his advertisements in *Bell's Life* and the *Sporting Gazette* were promising as much. The second *Almanack* was vastly superior to the first. Having provided a complete set of All England v United England and Gentlemen v Players scorecards in the 1864 edition, Wisden now prepared a set of Oxford v Cambridge scores, plus a Gentlemen v Players match he had forgotten first time round. Wisden also included sections on Parr's England team in Australia, MCC's major matches in 1864, and on all eight of the first-class counties. Already, the *Almanack* of today was taking shape.

All the frivolous add-ons – knur and spell, canals, the Wars of the Roses – were expunged. This was now strictly a cricketer's book. A. H. Baily & Co. may have been spooked, since there was no second edition of the *Cricket Chronicle*. Fred Lillywhite, editor of the *Guide to Cricketers*, was rather more than spooked. To address the threat of the *Almanack*, he had prepared sections on rackets, golf, bowls, quoits and rowing – just as Wisden was removing them.

Edward Pawsey, aged 13, was convicted of wilful damage to a wall at the cricket ground in Bury St Edmunds. The mayor ordered the delinquent to pay a fine of 2s 2d, plus 7s 6d costs. The money not being forthcoming, the lad was sent to gaol for seven days. — *Bury and Norwich Post*, 4 October

He evidently did not see Wisden's devotion to full county scorecards coming, and stuck with his potted scores.

Fred was dealt a further blow on 12 October, when *Sporting Life* announced that John Lillywhite – his older brother – planned to launch his own *Cricketers' Companion* in the spring. It would include coaching guides for batsmen and bowlers, and lengthy match reports on every first-class game in 1864, though without full scorecards (Wisden still preferred scorecards to match reports). Fred was so stunned that he did not manage to publish, as he usually did, an autumn edition of his *Guide*. He did not even advertise his 1865 edition until 11 March, by which time Wisden's second *Almanack* had been available for more than two months, and John's *Companion* was a mere fortnight away.

When the *Guide* finally arrived, after some delay, on 29 April, it caused consternation: Fred Lillywhite had been unable to prevent his bitterness spilling onto the page. His player profiles had been substantially amended. John Wisden's had not been especially complimentary to begin with:

> Wisden was one of the best bowlers that England ever produced, but it did not last so long as his celebrated predecessors. He can manage a few overs now, on the spot, but with little effect, having to attend to business, which fortunately was obtained and left to him, and for which he is as much distinguished as he is now a cricketer. He is the energetic secretary of the United England Eleven, and his diplomacy on all subjects of match-making is, it is believed, acknowledged to be equal to the late veteran Clarke.

But the 1865 revision pulled no punches:

> Was a good 'un, but now does nothing for his county, England, or any other eleven, in fact, devotes his time to do a 'deal of good' for promoting the manly game, for which he spends a vast amount of coin, being a paid secretary to the Cricketers' Fund Society, chairman (in daily attendance) Mr. Thomas Box, late of the Brighton ground. Wisden is

An illegal meeting of Irish separatists was held in Kilkenny, under the pretence of a cricket match. The numbers were estimated at 800, and several marched with a violin, fife and drum, and wore green hat-bands. No attempt was made at wild speaking. — *Londonderry Sentinel*, 7 October

> also the 'energetic' secretary to the United England Eleven, and expects an appointment to his county club.

Wisden was not the only target of Fred's ire. Fred felt several of his former cricketing friends had been conspiring with Wisden against him. He accused his brother John of "poaching for ideas on another field, without licence". He called George Tarrant "a very fast bowler – fast in every way", and was scathing in his assessment of George Parr: "His time is now devoted to other purposes, far from promoting the game of cricket. Was the able manager (when out of his bedroom) in America." For good measure, he wrote that Wisden's United England matches were "liable to degenerate into a listless farce with a result of no public interest whatever".

The consequences were predictably disastrous for Fred's reputation. While *The Era* was circumspect in its assessment ("We regret the tone employed in treating of some of the professionals of England"), the *Sporting Gazette* was not.

> The editor has stepped into the regions of abuse and personality only worthy of a Mississippi editor in a rage, with the additional drawback of being unable to rival a Mississippi editor in grammar or English. None can calculate the harm done to the cause of unity by this spiteful twaddle.

MCC withdrew its official support of the *Guide*, on the grounds that Fred Lillywhite had "exceeded the fair limits of criticism upon cricketers", while John's *Companion* secured the patronage of the Prince of Wales. Disgraced and despairing, Fred quit his London premises, and returned to Brighton. In September 1866, after the 22nd and final edition of his *Guide* – in which all the snide remarks had been removed – he died, aged 38. "Let his faults be buried with his bones," wrote *Sporting Life*.

A number of boys were playing cricket on the moor, when one, Henry Coles, having been called names by another, James McCoskrie, became irritated and struck him a terrific blow on the nose, which caused the blood to flow and blackened both his eyes. Coles claimed that McCoskrie had first struck him with the bat, but the chairman was unconvinced, and ruled that Coles should be fined 13 shillings. — *Langport and Somerton Herald*, 8 October

The school cricket season – to which John was to devote a hefty chunk of his *Companion* – finally came to an end on the first Saturday in October. That night, at Tiverton, a gentleman named Jarman was hastening to catch the last train when he claimed to have been set upon by ten "overgrown lads" of Blundell's School, armed with cricket bats. He had seen them off with his walking stick, but rather than contacting the police, he wrote an angry letter to the *Tiverton Gazette*. There was a stiff reply, from one of the masters: "I can confidently assert that there have not been ten bats at the school for at least two years. In any case, what could ten boys be doing with cricket bats at night-time?" Then, for good measure: "I understand that Mr. Jarman is a man of small stature. He must also be a mighty hero to disperse ten armed men merely by the free use of his stick."

The last first-class game of the year took place at Newmarket from 6 to 8 October; no county game has ever begun later in a season. It was to have been a fourth North v South fixture, which would have broken the 1–1 tie, but the Cambridgeshire players' refusal to travel to Islington for the third rankled with many of the Southerners. For Newmarket, 18 of the North's players made themselves available – compared with only two from the South. Several accepted invitations to appear in a professionals' XI at Islington, against a gentlemen's XXII assembled by the ubiquitous Charles Absolon. That did not prove much of an alternative: the pros made 169, and the gentlemen were eight down before they scored a run; in the follow-on, the professionals sympathetically brought on their wicketkeeper, Pooley, to bowl, but even he was too hard to handle, and he reeled in 11 wickets.

To prevent a mismatch at Newmarket, the match was refashioned as Cambridge and Yorkshire v Kent and Nottinghamshire. But it was a bowlers'

> After the game, some of the Underwood team went to a dancing-room. Joseph Haynes arrived in search of his son, who had played in the match, but upon going into the room his hat was seized by a man by the name of Bostock, who put it on his head and jumped onto a table. In doing so, he damaged Mr. Haynes's hat. The case was settled by Bostock agreeing to pay half the cost of a new hat. — *Nottingham Journal*, 10 October

pitch, and the Kentish curse spread to the Nottingham men: they were all out for 84 and 57. *Sporting Life* reported a "nondescript match" and a poor attendance, which was attributed to Newmarket "not really being a cricketing place". Such excuses masked the growing discontent among the professionals – at least for a few weeks.

There was no method of deciding the county champions in the mid-nineteenth century. The *Maidstone Journal* had used the expression ahead of the Kent v Nottinghamshire game of 1837, both teams having beaten Sussex, and a knockout competition had been mooted in 1855 but, in general, the manner of assessment was purely qualitative. At the end of the 1864 season, the sporting press had their say.

> **Cambridgeshire** played only three matches, but won all three, and if winning every match does not place a county A1 among the cricketing shires, we don't know what does.
>
> **Surrey** had a stirring and splendid hitting time. That their season would have been so much more interesting had they played Cambridgeshire there can be no doubt. Nevertheless, 1864 has been a successful and memorable season. The astounding fact that considerably over 100,000 persons paid for admission at The Oval during the season affords incontrovertible evidence that where good pitches are provided, the public will congregate.
>
> Although **Middlesex** are a young club, they have a lot of old stagers, and they laboured under the usual disadvantages of a newly-formed organisation: a paucity of professional talent. The new pavilion at Islington, though, is paid for, and there is a good balance at the bank.
>
> **Sussex** are unquestionably looking up. The old professionals were all there, and well backed up by young hands; James Lillywhite has become a star in the bowling line. Bowling of such calibre will go a long way towards bringing Sussex once more to the topmost round of the ladder.

The rectory of Prittlewell has been given by the Bishop to his nephew. This young man has crusaded against choral music, cricket and beards. It proves what tolerance a family connection can bring about, since the Bishop indulges frequently in cricket. — *Lincolnshire Chronicle*, 14 October

> When we consider the high character of some of **Nottinghamshire's** cricket, and that the county has steered clear of those abominations – drawn matches – we come to the conclusion that they have played a good and tolerably successful season.
>
> The present **Yorkshire** bowlers are the best county attack in England. In first-class matches, they bowled 5,691 balls, and not a single wide. But in terms of unity with itself, the Yorkshire club is to be deplored. The York club wished to take over as headquarters from Sheffield, whose committee understandably refused, and there was no co-operation between the gentlemen and the professionals, who insisted, uniquely among the first-class counties, in maintaining two distinct clubs.
>
> If any team's form exemplified the glorious uncertainty of cricket, it was **Hampshire's**. Her strength being for the most part amateur, it could hardly be expected that she would pull off many matches against clubs with a preponderance of professional talent.
>
> **Kent** had a bad time of it. The county's professionals were not especially brilliant in batting, and Mr. Fryer's inability to keep wicket was a material loss. There is need of a full-time county ground, and the answer is undoubtedly the beautiful and accessible facility at Crystal Palace, which the committee must embrace as the club's headquarters.

None of these end-of-term reports went as far as identifying a champion, though the two contenders were clearly Surrey and Cambridgeshire. Even so, the oldest known identification of a champion dates back to this very year. After Surrey enjoyed a superlative summer in 1886, the following year's *Almanack* wrote: "there can be no question that the county occupies a higher position in the cricket world today than it has done at any time since the memorable season of 1864, when the team went through the whole summer without losing a single eleven-a-side match". The cricket historian Rowland Bowen, writing in the 1959 *Almanack*, used this reference to suggest the 1864 Surrey team were the inaugural county champions. He repeated this, rather more assertively, in the 1963 edition,

> The well-known Sussex cricketer George Wells, a dealer in cricketing materials, has been declared bankrupt at Brighton. His debts amount to a total of £552, and his principal creditor is Mr. Page, bat-maker at The Oval, to whom he owes the sum of £330. — *Sussex Advertiser*, 18 October

and from then on, the Almanack carried a list of county champions – with no caveats or footnotes – starting with Surrey in 1864. The distinction between Bowen's winners and the *actual* champions was finally made clear in the 1990s.

The absence of a Surrey v Cambridgeshire match, which would have made clear which were the better side, was lamented by the newspapers. The *Maidstone Journal* was a peculiar exception, faithfully reporting in mid-June that "the match between Surrey and Cambrideshire [sic] at Lord's was drawn on Saturday evening last, the numbers being Cambridgeshire 266 and 384, against which Surrey obtained 416 and 28 for the loss of one wicket". This sounds like a thrilling match, and it was a great pity that it never took place at all. The *Maidstone Journal* had published a completely false report.

There is some evidence that Cambridgeshire might have been superior to Surrey. They beat Yorkshire twice, while Surrey had to make do with a draw at Sheffield. Using the 2026 points system in the County Championship, and calculating the average per game, Cambridgeshire would have finished first.

	P	W	L	D	Pts	Avge
Cambridgeshire	3	3	0	0	48	16.0
Surrey	8	6	0	2	112	14.0
Middlesex	4	3	1	0	48	12.0
Sussex	8	5	2	1	88	11.0
Nottinghamshire	7	3	4	0	48	6.9
Yorkshire	7	2	4	1	40	5.7
Hampshire	4	0	4	0	0	0.0
Kent	7	0	7	0	0	0.0

Factoring in modern batting and bowling bonus points – notwithstanding that the totals after 110 overs were not recorded (and that these were four-ball

Michael McIntyre, the Nottinghamshire fast bowler, was assaulted at Greasley by a drunken and riotous John Burrows, and a fight ensued. The Reverend E. Cayley, of Brinsley, came to the spot, and the row soon finished. Burrows claimed McIntyre had knocked him down and injured his knee severely, but was fined 22s 6d. — *Nottingham Journal*, 31 October overs) – Cambridgeshire would still have been top, with an average of 19 to Surrey's 18.6. They may only have played three games, but with a perfect record, and such a good write-up in the press, they seem hard done by in Bowen's final analysis. But Cambridgeshire had done themselves no favours by refusing to play home-and-away fixtures with Surrey, Kent or Sussex, apparently on the basis that the travel expenses were too great. As *Sporting Life* somewhat tartly pointed out, they had managed to find the money to go to Lord's to play Nottinghamshire. This, like the Islington and Newmarket fixtures, only served to highlight the growing rift between the professionals of north and south.

NOVEMBER

A geographical divide between two teams had caused problems enough – but by November, the United England team itself was divided. In all but three of their 13 seasons, they had played more matches in the north than in the south. And while they no longer had to fulfil matches in Scotland, as they had in the team's heyday, the southerners did not relish their mid-September trips to chilly Bradford and Halifax. The haughty attitude of Cambridgeshire and the arguments over the Islington and Newmarket games had evidently become too much for John Lillywhite and Ned Willsher who, on 10 November, formed a breakaway team: the United South of England.

The identity of the new team's founders said much about the impact of the rift. Lillywhite was the umpire who, two years earlier, had no-balled Willsher for bowling overarm. There was no love lost between them. But they joined forces to stage a meeting at the Bridge House Hotel, opposite London Bridge station, and signed up Lockyer, Caesar, Mortlock, Griffith, Sewell, Humphrey and Jupp from Surrey, Bennett from Kent, Hearne from Middlesex, and Lillywhite's cousin James from Sussex. Several of the men immediately wrote "Dear John" letters to Wisden, resigning from the United England team. *Bell's Life* wrote that "the appearance of so many cracks caused no little commotion", and the *Sporting Gazette* worried about the future.

> We have known for some time that this was in progress, but we can and do write that we publish it with regret, because we would rather see professional cricketers burying past differences – and thus becoming more truly united. Whether there will be a sufficient demand to fully employ three crack elevens is a moot question. And how about that fine annual match at Lord's? What is to become of the contest?

Robert Williams and James Bowden were charged with drunken and riotous behaviour. Williams pleaded guilty, and said he was sorry, but he had a game of cricket at Dunster that afternoon, then went out with the band, and had too much cider. He was fined five shillings. Bowden did not appear, and was sentenced to a week's imprisonment. — *Western Times*, 12 November

Wisden called what was left of the United Eleven together at Gregory's Hotel – not in the north of England, but in central London, somewhat ironically – to discuss which new players they might recruit. No definite choices were made at that meeting, but in the event, they signed up Greenwood, Pryor, Reynolds and Thewlis. They were decent players, but hardly sufficient to make up for those who had quit, and as soon as 1865 the United Eleven were clearly in decline: they lost by an innings to Lansdown, for whom three Graces played and shared all the wickets; Teddy scored 121.

The new United South of England side started 1865 strongly, but lost three games on the trot to Christ Church College, Accrington and Hertford, then suffered two more defeats at the end of the season, St Albans skittling them for 52, and a Gentlemen of Surrey side – somewhat dubiously including Teddy Grace, who chalked up twin fifties and 13 wickets – thrashing them by 155 runs.

The Graces eventually threw in their lot with the United South of England men, but Gilbert later reflected that 1864 marked the beginning of the end. Division followed division, and soon there were a United North of England Eleven, then a United North and South of England Eleven, followed by a New United South of England Eleven. The Lord's game, for so long a flagship fixture, was last played in 1866, and not long afterwards there were estimated to be as many as 19 professional touring sides in England. One by one, they died out, until – somewhat poetically – the only one remaining was All England, the team who had started it all.

Several teams continued to play well into mid-autumn. *Bell's Weekly Messenger* suggested that some "enthusiastic votaries of cricket", if they had their way, would prolong the season to Christmas. Charles Absolon wrapped

> The aldermen discussed the damage to Woodhouse Moor. It was observed that cricketers had repeatedly been taken before the magistrates and fined, but when men of substance, who exercised their horses on the turf, had been before the justices, they had got off scot-free. This was not felt to be a dignified position for the council. — *Leeds Times*, 12 November

up his season by playing in an invitation XI that took on (and lost to) three professionals: Humphrey, Jupp and Pooley. In Scotland, Mrs. Blair was enjoying her celebrity, and had taken to presenting a new bat to the highest scorer in each Inchmartine game. After the closing match, which gave the club a 100% success record for 1864, she gave a short speech. "It is almost needless to mention that suitable refreshments were served in abundance," wrote the *Dundee Advertiser*.

Most clubs held an end-of-season dinner after their final fixture. Some sort of prizegiving was usually in order, and the Yorkshire club of Tapton presented some unusual awards: "a very handsome electro-plated tea-pot, value 15s" to the player of the year, "a patent garden syringe" to the batsman with the best average, and "a pair of handsome carvers" to the bowler with the best average. The bowler with the second-best average received a case of razors. East Gawber, a short distance to the north, followed their meal with drinks at a local inn. "The evening was spent in singing," reported the *Barnsley Chronicle*, "but when returning to their homes not one inebriate was found".

When Burton Joyce played Carlton on 7 November, the *Nottinghamshire Journal* lamented the continuation of the season: "There was sufficient interest centred in this match to cause its being played, despite the threatenings of bronchitis. The bowlers, batters and fielders kept on overcoats owing to the bitter coldness." The final recorded game of 1864 took place on Friday 25 November, between the Lincolnshire villages of Marton and Normanby. It was agreed that a single-innings game should be played until sunset, and Normanby made sure there would be a positive result by being tumbled out for 33. Marton had the rest of the day to bat, and after an early wobble, the Sleightholme brothers conjured one of the more unusual scorecards of the season.

MARTON

Wildsmith b West	0
Hugill b West	0
Dowson c Sanderson b West	4
R. Sleightholme not out	44
J. Sleightholme not out	128
Extras	15
Total	**191**

So ended the most eventful English cricketing summer in history. *Wisden Cricketers' Almanack* had made its first appearance, the first full-strength England team to tour Australia had returned triumphant, overarm bowling had been legalised, Lord's had been saved from destruction, county cricket had been born again, and W. G. Grace had made his first headline-grabbing appearances. It was a year like no other.

> "Cricket may be said to have ended for the season, and a sadly lifeless one it has been." — *Illustrated London News*

DECEMBER

The English season may have been over, but cricket was – even in 1864 – an all-year game. By December, the Australian season was under way, with club matches all over Melbourne and Sydney. The *Australia and New Zealand Gazette* was optimistic.

> Our cricketers are now wakening into activity again, as the season for field sports sets in. Many of the clubs, in city and country, have held their annual meetings, and are now doing whatever they can to muster and increase their forces. There is no prospect of the 1864-65 season being distinguished by an England tour, but we are promised what is next-best – or, as many think, better – a resumption of contests between New South Wales and Victoria.

The sport was also thriving in New Zealand. When Parr's tourists had made land near Dunedin on 31 January, Otago had just defeated Canterbury in a three-day game at the South Dunedin Recreation Ground. This would later be designated New Zealand's first first-class fixture. The Otago team included five who had played first-class cricket for Victoria: John Jacomb, from Tasmania; brothers Christopher and John Mace, and James Redfearn, all from Yorkshire; and Surrey-born Richard Coulston. Canterbury were markedly inferior to Otago with bat and ball, though they did have Augustus Eatwell Tennant, soon to score runs against the English. The only member of either team known to have been born in New Zealand was Gibson Turton, who batted at ten and did not bowl.

By December 1864, the New Zealanders were back on the field, not just in Otago and Canterbury, but in Marlborough, Nelson, Wellington and Southland. Canterbury improved rapidly enough to beat Otago in New Zealand's second first-class game, at the beginning of 1865.

> Harry Hall, the well-known Nottingham professional cricketer, died at that town on Thursday. The poor fellow, who was greatly respected, had long been suffering from erysipelas. — *Sporting Life*, 3 December

Club cricket, played by civilian residents and natives – as opposed to military matches, staged between garrisoned soldiers and navy crews – was, by the end of 1864, firmly established in several places. Though almost a decade would pass before an England team reprised the USA and Canada tour of 1859, numerous American clubs were still playing regularly, including three in New York. *Bell's Life*, though, was not convinced that cricket would enjoy a long life there.

> The England tour of late 1859, it was hoped, would have given a stir to Americans in cricket, but still baseball dominates. The main excuse is the want of a good ground to practise and play cricket upon. Then there is the fact that a cricket match takes all day to play, and time is money in this country. Baseball rarely exceeds 3½ hours. In some instances, no persuasion or argument can induce an employer to believe that recreation is even necessary. The best place for cricket is the St George's Club, delightfully situated at Hoboken, a ground expressly made for the great England match of 1859. The club consists principally of Englishmen, some of whom are naturalised, but there are also several bona fide Americans. They suffered only one defeat in 1864, to the Young Americans Club of Philadelphia. The East New York and Willow Clubs have a ground at Bedford, on Long Island.

In Europe, club cricket was by no means confined to France; Paris just received the most attention because of the visits by Nottingham and Warwickshire Knickerbockers. Hamburg took on Frankfurt, without any obviously German participants, but this did not deter the two clubs from assembling an official Germany team to play France, who won by an innings and 42 runs. The Italian cities of Livorno and Florence played home and away to huge crowds, who were attracted by the novelty (Florence won the first match, and the second was drawn). *Bell's Life* found three clubs in Belgium, at Antwerp, Ostend and Tienen – where 23 of the 30 players were natives.

Clubs were also springing up all around Asia. The Freemasons formed a club in Sri Lanka (then Ceylon), as did the residents of Trincomalee. Hong Kong had the Taepings and the Imperialists. But India, by some margin, was the epicentre of Asian cricket: even in 1864, there were too many clubs to keep track of. There were reports of matches involving Bangalore and Dharwad in

December. A fixture between combined clubs – Knuckles and Valley versus Lagalla and Matelle – was reported by *Bell's Life* without the slightest hint of where any of them might be located. The *Lahore Civil and Military Gazette* was diligent in reporting games of almost any standard. By its own admission, "Cricket, concerts and slandering our neighbours are our only amusements," though by mid-December it had toned down its enthusiasm: "Of late, so much has been said about cricketing in all the up-country papers, that we are unwilling to inflict upon our readers a full report of the match."

Even so, the *Gazette* continued to cover fixtures as far flung as the Himalayan foothills ("The Nanital fielding was very good – but Bareilly were very bad") and present-day Pakistan.

> A session judge was umpiring a match at Lahore, and a knotty point was presented for his decision at a moment when, though apparently regarding the wicket with earnest attention, his thoughts were upon the Bench. Startled by the brisk demand, "How is that, Umpire?" the dispenser of Right slowly pronounced from the depths of his moral unconsciousness these words of Hindi: "Paanch saal kee jel!" [Five years' imprisonment!]

The British fort at Asirgarh – the Gibraltar of the East, besieged by the Imperial army in 1819 – had become a hotbed of cricketing activity to rival Calcutta and Madras. Two matches were staged between Asirgarh and 'The World', which included a mid-afternoon break for tiffin.

The soldiers of the Empire were also at it in China, where the Shanghai Garrison lost to a team of civilians, and at Gibraltar and Malta, where Britain's finest evidently did little other than organise fixtures against each other. The Malta men were given a tough time when HMS *St George* came, bringing a

His Honour heard a case relating to a cricket match between Grindleford and Leadmill for a new cricket ball, value 6s 6d. The umpire of one team gave one of the opposing batters out, and a dispute arose, which resulted in the batting team drawing up the stumps and going home. The parties, being unable to settle the matter, made recourse to the County Court to determine the winner. The case was thrown out. — *Sheffield Independent*, 15 December sailor named Pearson, who scored an unbeaten 127. No one else in the match passed 18.

Cricket was played wherever the British Navy made land. In Greece, a team from the Zante Garrison beat a scratch side assembled from the officers of HMS *Cossack* and *Trident*, then sailed to Kefalonia, and defeated a team from the garrison there.

In Uruguay, HMS *Bombay* played HMS *Satellite* at Montevideo, and the top-scorer in both Satellite innings, with 16 and 42, was C. W. Chute, a noted Sevenoaks Vine player. The men of the *Bombay* then got a match together in Brazil, and by the time the year was out, the São Paulo Railway Company – largely staffed by British expatriates – boasted two teams of its own.

Another team of expats, in Peru, beat HMS *Leander* by an innings, with five of the crew – perhaps a little overstretched by shore-leave refreshment – being run out second time around. A combined side from HMS *Princess Royal* and *Orontes* lost heavily in Cape Town to a team calling themselves South Africa, comprising nine Boers and two missionaries. The *Dublin Daily Express* was particularly impressed by that.

> We can imagine the enthusiasm which a game must occasion to our colonial friends, and can almost realise their feelings when thoughts wander, fancy free, over the few thousand miles which sever them from the cricket fields of boyhood, to the old country – until they are recalled to life by hearing the shouts "Well caught, Watermeyer!" or "Well hit, Schimper!", names so indicative of their origin as to transplant them once more to African soil. It is pleasant to record the progress of the noble game in South Africa. It is a game which tends greatly to reduce or prevent obesity, an infliction much prevailing in the Cape.

It wasn't just the Navy boats who brought cricket, either. When Prince Alfred, brother of the Prince of Wales, undertook a fishing expedition to Norway, his entourage improvised a match in the Lofoten Islands.

Cricket had also taken hold in the Caribbean, though the black population initially had no stake in it. Jamaica had the two most active clubs, Kingston and Surrey, who faced each other at least twice a year. According to the *Jamaica Dispatch*, their first match of 1864 threatened to be acrimonious in the extreme.

> Kingston had recruited seven good players from the British military. The Surrey captain refused to start the game unless they were omitted, but the Kingston captain refused to start unless they played. Having already accepted the challenge, Surrey had no alternative but to proceed. They were without one of their best bats, and their excellent long-stop, but somehow managed to earn a draw.

The teams met again in November, when Kingston won, and cordial relations were restored. Jamaica would have been the most likely location for the beginning of first-class cricket in the West Indies, but for its distance from the other three cricketing territories: Barbados, Trinidad (both about 1,200 miles away) and Guyana (1,500 miles away, on the South American coast). The accolade went to the Garrison Savannah, just east of Bridgetown in Barbados, on 15 February 1865.

Barbados were captained by Frederick Smith, whose brother Augustus opened the batting and bowling alongside him, and whose nephew Sydney went on to play for Northamptonshire. All the Barbados team had been born on the island – a stark contrast with New Zealand's first-class debutants a year earlier. The visitors were Guyana (then known as Demerara), a disparate bunch including a Vincentian, Henry Beresford, and a Nottinghamshire man, Frederick Bury. No batsman reached double-figures in either Demerara innings, and the Smiths shared 18 wickets. But within a couple of seasons, Demerara were beating not only Barbados, but Trinidad too. Jamaica had to wait 30 years for first-class cricket.

West Indian cricket, by the end of 1864, was no longer an expat game. Of the pioneers at Garrison Savannah, Bury alone was born outside the Caribbean. Only he would have been unaccustomed to the humidity and heat. Like George Parr, the English captain who spent the first days of 1864 acclimatising to a Melbourne heatwave, Bury was born in Radcliffe-on-Trent. Neither could have

> George Tarrant, the celebrated professional, brought a case against a publican named King, to recover £5 for money lent. The hearing took an unexpected turn. On learning that King earned as much as £2 a week, by serving short measures to the drinkers at The Lion, the judge ordered him to be committed for 20 days. — *Cambridge Independent Press,* 17 December

dreamed, as a boy, where life would take them, and in what unlikely locations they would be able to play cricket, even while England was amid a winter freeze.

On Boxing Day – the final Monday of 1864 – the *Leeds Times* reported that a cricket match was played on ice, at the Moor Dam in Yeadon, between eleven with skates and eleven without. Just as Parr cannot have imagined his cricketing voyages across the seas, ice cricket in England is unimaginable now. But then, the past is a foreign country. They play cricket differently there.

1864 SEASON
LEADING FIRST-CLASS BATSMEN

	M	I	NO	R	HS	100	50	Avge
W. Mortlock	18	25	0	855	105	1	6	34.20
H. H. Stephenson	15	25	4	824	119	2	3	39.23
H. Jupp	16	28	3	647	110	1	2	25.88
T. Humphrey	14	24	1	602	94	0	5	26.17
T. Hearne	18	28	3	562	125	1	3	22.48
R. Daft	11	20	1	498	80	0	4	26.21
G. Griffith	17	27	2	489	86*	0	3	19.56
G. Bennett	15	27	0	480	73	0	2	17.77
G. M. Kelson	14	27	0	446	83	0	2	16.51
T. Sewell	21	33	9	414	55	0	1	17.25
J. Grundy	18	31	4	389	36	0	0	14.40
T. Lockyer	16	21	1	375	108*	1	1	18.75
T. Hayward	8	12	0	355	66	0	2	29.58
J. Thewlis	10	20	1	348	77	0	2	18.31
G. Wells	10	15	2	345	82	0	3	26.53
G. Wootton	20	36	8	344	60	0	1	12.28
T. Case	9	13	0	339	116	1	0	26.07
C. Brampton	10	19	0	333	82	0	2	17.52
C. H. Ellis	13	18	1	333	54	0	2	19.58
R. Iddison	13	23	0	330	44	0	0	14.34
J. Rowbotham	12	23	0	307	57	0	1	13.34
John Lillywhite	9	14	2	301	64	0	2	25.08
T. Bignall	12	23	1	300	49	0	0	13.63
E. Willsher	16	30	3	288	37*	0	0	10.66
R. P. Carpenter	8	11	1	270	52	0	1	27.00
J. S. Frederick	9	15	0	268	44	0	0	17.86
H. E. Bull	8	15	0	267	46	0	0	17.80
J. Caesar	9	13	2	267	132*	1	0	24.27
J. Berry	8	14	1	266	42	0	0	20.46
James Lillywhite	12	17	2	264	105	1	0	17.60
C. H. Smith	8	13	2	255	95	0	1	23.18
G. Anderson	6	11	5	255	99*	0	1	42.50
E. W. Tritton	12	19	0	252	110	1	0	13.26
C. G. Lyttelton	4	7	0	241	128	1	1	34.42
J. Jackson	10	17	1	237	68*	0	2	14.81
R. A. H. Mitchell	6	9	1	237	103	1	1	29.62

1864 SEASON
LEADING FIRST-CLASS BOWLERS

	B	M	R	W	BB	10	5	Avge
J. Grundy	3506	412	1109	99	9-19	10	2	11.31
G. Wootton	3516	357	1277	87	8-15	5	2	15.02
James Lillywhite	3239	333	1145	83	6-25	10	2	13.79
E. Willsher	3486	386	1065	79	7-47	6	0	13.48
G. Griffith	2730	205	1140	69	6-32	6	1	16.52
G. F. Tarrant	1610	134	590	67	7-30	8	4	8.80
T. Sewell	2655	258	909	50	6-64	4	0	18.18
W. F. Maitland	1117	77	521	48	8-48	4	2	11.84
G. Bennett	1645	121	824	45	7-68	2	0	18.31
V. E. Walker	1054	71	519	42	9-63	4	2	12.35
T. Hearne	1918	215	653	41	6-37	2	0	16.32
R. Iddison	1008	51	550	37	6-38	2	0	14.86
R. C. Tinley	926	36	508	35	6-49	4	1	14.51
W. Mortlock	1213	54	688	32	7-42	2	0	21.50
W. Shepherd	1457	134	596	31	8-49	2	0	19.22
C. H. Ellis	1072	40	600	30	5-67	2	0	20.00
R. D. Walker	1287	129	534	29	6-76	2	1	18.41
G. R. Atkinson	1644	128	559	29	6-22	1	0	19.27
W. Slinn	1148	113	447	27	6-19	2	1	16.55
W. H. Fryer	1170	121	416	26	8-40	1	0	16.00
I. Hodgson	1506	187	472	23	4-61	0	0	20.52
J. Jackson	1196	126	377	22	3-17	0	0	17.13
H. Arkwright	484	32	279	21	9-79	3	1	13.28
L. Greenwood	1107	139	347	18	5-46	1	0	19.27
F. R. Reynolds	590	66	185	17	4-22	0	0	10.88
W. Catling	328	23	131	16	5-29	1	0	8.18
T. Lockyer	530	40	238	15	6-44	1	0	15.86
G. M. Kelson	898	67	462	15	4-35	0	0	30.80
T. Hayward	368	32	163	14	6-72	1	0	11.64
A. Shaw	582	67	219	14	6-31	1	0	15.64
R. Fillery	756	59	334	14	5-40	1	0	23.85
T. S. Curteis	605	81	162	13	4-23	0	0	12.46
A. S. Teape	345	34	114	12	6-41	1	0	10.36
F. G. Pelham	497	47	175	12	5-43	1	0	14.58
E. F. Dyke	189	21	41	10	6-14	1	1	4.10
T. Harris	348	18	184	10	6-81	1	0	18.40

W. G. GRACE IN 1864

Date	Match	Runs		Wickets	
28 May	Hanham v Mr. Messenger's XI at Frenchay	36*	15	6	0
2 Jun	Clifton v Bedminster at Durdham Down	3	–	6	1
9 Jun	Clifton v Clifton College at Durdham Down	3*		–	
11 Jun	Hanham v Stapleton at Pudway Hill	20		8	
25 Jun	Stapleton v Derham Bros. at Durdham Down	9	29	2	6
30 Jun	All England v Eighteen of Lansdown at Bath (3 days)	15*		–	
6 Jul	Clifton v Lansdown at Bath (2 days)	38	0	2	6
8 Jul	G. G. Sharp's XI v Knole Park at Knole Park	5		6	7
11 Jul	South Wales v Surrey at The Oval (2 days)	5	38	4	1
14 Jul	South Wales v Gentlemen of Sussex at Hove (3 days)	170	56*	2	0
18 Jul	**16th birthday**				
19 Jul	W. Gloucestershire v Knole Park at Knole Park (2 days)	4	39	–	
21 Jul	South Wales v MCC at Lord's	50	2	1	0
25 Jul	South Wales v Knickerbockers at Islington	18		4	
27 Jul	South Wales v Southgate at Southgate	14	1*	–	
28 Jul	South Wales v I Zingari at Lord's (2 days)	34	47	2	
30 Jul	Hanham v Weston-super-Mare at Weston	15	78	3	
2 Aug	Clifton v Mr Baber's XXII at Durdham Down (2 days)	11	4	1	4
4 Aug	Lansdown v Wiltshire Wanderers at Bath	29		–	
5 Aug	Lansdown v Wiltshire Wanderers at Bath	4	7	–	
6 Aug	Stapleton v Bristol Schoolmasters at Bristol	28	21*	6	3
8 Aug	Clifton v Fownes's XI at Durdham Down	126		1	6
10 Aug	Clifton v Lansdown at Durdham Down (2 days)	19	4	1	
13 Aug	Hanham v Stapleton at Hanham	18		5	6
15 Aug	Clifton v Universities XI at Durdham Down (2 days)	30	14*	3	6
20 Aug	Hanham v Frenchay at Frenchay	28	27*	7	8
22 Aug	Mr. Harley's XI v Mr. Muttlebury's XI at Weston	58		5	3
23 Aug	W. Gloucestershire v Bowood at Bowood (2 days)	18	3	–	
27 Aug	Stapleton v Bristol Schoolmasters at Fishponds	0	5	6	5
31 Aug	Frenchay v Long Ashton at Frenchay	51		2	2
31 Aug	Frenchay v Long Ashton at Frenchay (beer match)		*unknown*		
9 Sep	Clifton v Bristol Grammar School XXII at Clifton	15		12	15
17 Sep	Hanham v Bitton at Hanham	3	10	5	6
28 Sep	W. Gloucestershire v Cheltenham Coll. at Cheltenham	29		1	3

33 matches · 1,306 runs · average 29.68 · 2 hundreds · 5 fifties
189 wickets · 21 five-wicket hauls · 37 catches · 2 stumpings

PARR'S TWELVE IN AUSTRALIA

	M	I	R	HS	Avge	50	W	BB
G. Anderson	13	17	177	38	11.06	–		
J. Caesar	17	23	217	40	9.86	–	9	6-31
W. Caffyn	19	26	475	43	19.00	–	32	5-11
R. P. Carpenter	19	26	447	121	18.62	2 *		
A. Clarke	16	21	151	40	7.55	–		
E. M. Grace	24	33	538	106	16.81	1 *	31	7-4
T. Hayward	18	25	398	61	16.58	–	118	15-34
J. Jackson	20	26	238	45	9.53	–	151	11-22
T. Lockyer	19	25	315	44	15.00	–	1	
G. Parr	14	18	247	65	16.46	1		
G. F. Tarrant	23	31	340	41	10.96	–	102	12-29
R. C. Tinley	19	23	156	24	9.75	–	284	14-22

Also batted: G. Marshall 14 v Ararat.

* includes one hundred.

Impromptu matches are included. Bowling averages are excluded, since in many matches the runs conceded by each bowler were not recorded.

Parr's Eleven have now brought their Australian campaign to a close, and leave for England by the April mail. They have, one and all, proved themselves good men and true, and during their stay of four months in the colonies they have shown themselves worthy of their reputation. Much has been said about the competitive merits of the two Elevens which have visited Australia, but there cannot be a doubt in all unprejudiced minds that the Eleven now leaving these shores is greatly superior to anything the colonists have ever before seen in point of cricketing excellence. The previous Eleven showed nothing equal to the wicketkeeping of Lockyer, the batting of Hayward and Carpenter, or the bowling of Jackson, Tarrant and Tinley, and it is more than probable that the Eleven which first visited Australia would now find their match in a Victorian XXII. A Victorian team never worked better in the field than that which met Parr's Eleven in the farewell match, and it has been noticed that in each match in which the Englishmen have been engaged with a Victorian XXII they have been compelled to play a thoroughly defensive game. The visit of this Eleven will be productive of much benefit to colonial cricketers, if from no other cause by its having led to the retention of Caffyn, the best all-round man among them; and, with the aid of such a coach, Victoria will doubtless in future intercolonial matches take her proper position.

— The *Melbourne Age*, quoted in Wisden's *Cricketer's Almanack* for 1865

THE LAWS OF CRICKET IN 1864

compared with the 2026 Code of Laws

I. The ball was the same weight as today, but could be a fraction larger, up to 9¼ inches in circumference.

II. The dimensions of the bat were the same.

III. The wicket was 27 inches high, and 8 inches wide – in both cases, an inch smaller than today.

IV. The bowling crease, between the two return creases, was 6 feet 8 inches wide; today, this is 8 feet 8 inches.

V. The popping crease was the same.

VI. The length of the pitch was the same.

VII. The pitch could not be covered during a match.

VIII. The pitch could be relocated after rain.

IX. An over contained four balls.

X. No-balls were called if, at the moment of delivery, bowlers threw or "jerked" the ball, or had their bowling hand above shoulder height, or did not ground their back foot behind the bowling crease (today, the front foot must be grounded behind the popping crease).

XI. The bowler could instruct the non-striker to stand to either side of the wicket.

XII. Any ball above the striker's head was a wide.

XIII. The only mode of dismissal from a no-ball or wide was run out.

XIV. As today, the umpire began the match with a call of "play".

XV. Bowled, as today.

XVI. Caught, as today.

XVII. Stumped, as today.

XVIII. Hit wicket, as today.

XIX. Obstructed the field, as today.

XX. Hit the ball twice, as today.

XXI. Run out, as today.

XXII. Hit wicket, by any part of the striker's dress (now amalgamated into a single hit wicket law).

XXIII. Handled the ball, as it was until 2017.

XXIV. Leg before wicket required the ball to pitch in line with the two wickets. Today, it may pitch outside off stump.

XXV. During a run-out, the decision as to which batter was dismissed was the same as today.

XXVI. No runs were scored when a catch is made, as today.

XXVII. Completed runs before a run out were counted, as today.

XXVIII. There were no boundaries; a fielder could call "lost ball", which gave the batters six runs, unless they had already run more.

XXIX. Dead ball, as it was until 2026 (the ball had to settle in the hands of the bowler or wicketkeeper).

XXX. Retired out, as today.

XXXI. Runners, as today.

XXXII. The batting team's captain had to agree on who could act as a fielding substitute, and where they would field.

XXXIII. Illegal fielding penalty, as today.

XXXIV. Striker legally protecting the wicket, as today.

XXXV. Position of the wicketkeeper, as today.

XXXVI. Unfair play had few exemplars; the umpires were expected to judge each situation on its merits.

XXXVII. The toss, as today.

XXXVIII. Timed out, interval between innings, and forfeitures, as today. Declarations were not permitted.

XXXIX. Appeals, as today.

XL. The umpire to call "no-ball" – but there was no signal.

XLI. The umpire to call "one short" – but there was no signal.

XLII. Umpires were not allowed to bet.

XLIII. Umpires could not be changed once a match had begun (unless found to have been betting).

XLIV. The umpire to call "over", as today.

XLV. The umpire to call "wide ball" – but there was no signal.

XLVI. The follow-on margin was 60 in a one-day game, and 80 in a multi-day game.

XLVII. "When one of the strikers shall have been put out, the use of the bat shall not be allowed to any person until the next striker shall come in."

INDEX

Excerpts from John Wisden's Cricketer's Almanack for 1864

The graces of the modern tea-table were quite unknown to the country-folk, although that favourite beverage, brought by the Dutch to Europe, was introduced into England by Lords Arlington and Ossary in 1666. It was not till nearly a century later that the middle classes of London and Edinburgh began to use tea daily. In the latter city, in the reigns of the Georges, tea was taken at four o'clock, and the meal was thence called "four hours".

MAYOR, the chief magistrate of a corporate town, called by the Saxons port-reeve; Henry Fitz-Alwyn was appointed first Mayor of London 1189; the style Right Honourable Lord was granted 1354; the Lord Mayor's Show was instituted 1453.

The first striking clock was erected at Westminster, 1368; the first correct time-keeper was set up at Hampton Court, 1540.

TRIAL OF CHARLES I. — On January 20, 1649, a tribunal, self-created and self-styled the High Court of Justice, met in Westminster Hall for the trial of the King. The Peers had refused to take any part in the proceedings. The members of the court, of whom about seventy sat in judgment, were taken chiefly from the army and the semblance of a Parliament then existing. A lawyer name Bradshaw was the president, and Coke acted as a solicitor for the nation. The King, brought from St. James's Palace, was placed within the bar, and then charged with tyranny, especially in waging war against his people. Never did Charles appear to more advantage than at this mockery of a trial. Summoning up all that kingly dignity of which he possessed no small share, he refused to be tried by a tribunal created in defiance of the laws. Where were the Peers? who alone by an ancient maxim of the Constitution could sit in judgment on a Peer. But all defence was useless, for the judges had already decided the matter among themselves. The case was spun out seven days, and then sentence of death was pronounced.

A brass bell weighing 17 cwt., cast in 1699, at Woolwich Arsenal, and used to call and disperse the labourers, was cleft by the hammer while ringing, from the effect of the severe frost on January 4, 1861.